❧THE COMPLETE❧
Mother
of the
Groom

THE COMPLETE

Mother
of the
Groom

HOW TO BE
GRACEFUL, HELPFUL,
AND HAPPY DURING
THIS SPECIAL TIME

SYDELL RABIN

Avon, Massachusetts

Published by
Adams Media, an F+W Media Company
57 Littlefield Street, Avon, MA 02322. U.S.A.
www.adamsmedia.com

ISBN 10: 1-59869-546-0
ISBN 13: 978-1-59869-546-5

Printed in the United States of America.

J I H G F E D C B A

Library of Congress Cataloging-in-Publication Data
is available from the publisher.

This publication is designed to provide accurate and authoritative information with regard to the subject matter covered. It is sold with the understanding that the publisher is not engaged in rendering legal, accounting, or other professional advice. If legal advice or other expert assistance is required, the services of a competent professional person should be sought.

—From a *Declaration of Principles* jointly adopted by a Committee of the American Bar Association and a Committee of Publishers and Associations

Many of the designations used by manufacturers and sellers to distinguish their product are claimed as trademarks. Where those designations appear in this book and Adams Media was aware of a trademark claim, the designations have been printed with initial capital letters.

This book is available at quantity discounts for bulk purchases.
For information, please call 1-800-289-0963.

Material from Chapters 2, 4, and 10 has previously appeared in *For the Bride* magazine. Material in Chapter 2 was the basis of the commentary essay "What Does She Call You?"on an NPR Mother's Day *Morning Edition.*

The names of women who have shared their stories with me, and those involved in their stories, have been changed in respect for their trust and privacy. The only name I have kept is Arnold, who is perfectly happy to be identified as the husband of the mother of the groom.

To my son and his wife,
who helped me to understand
the mother of the groom

Contents

Acknowledgments

LET ME BEGIN BY THANKING all the women—friends, relatives, and strangers—who so generously shared their experiences. Many of the stories were difficult for them to recount. Some came with tears. One shared with joy at finally becoming "visible." Most were eager to talk about a time that had been so mixed with pleasure and pain and kept so private until now.

I must thank my husband, Arnold, who persisted from the beginning when I was just keeping a journal about my son's wedding. "You've got a book in there," he insisted. He has not only been my most ardent fan and supporter but the best editor a writer could ever have.

And my thanks to Jonathan Revere, my Martha's Vineyard promoter and the producer/director of a weekly television interview program hosted by mystery writer Cynthia Riggs. He introduced me to Paula Munier of Adams Media via DVD interviews with each of us, and the mother of the groom found her voice.

INTRODUCTION

"Just Wear Beige, and Don't Say Anything"

BECAUSE EVERY BRIDAL COUPLE INVOLVES the mother of the groom, it is both startling and telling that so few books chronicle her adventure, confirm her feelings, and guide her through the prenuptial shoals. We know all about the father of the bride. He's a delightful character who pays the bills. The bride and her mother are followed every step of the way with articles, magazines, books, websites, and a whole industry of caterers, florists, photographers, and wedding gurus. The mother of the bride is harassed but patient, exhausted, and ultimately jubilant. The mother of the groom is often invisible.

However, there are real and practical ways for you to fit in and be part of this spectacular event. The making of a wedding need not always be the province of the bride's family. You are also a part of the wedding, and it's important that the bride and her family understand that the wedding is just as powerful a time in your family as it is in the bride's.

This book explores the practical, the personal, and the many other social issues that confront you from the months before the wedding to that very special day: the small and tender responses, the ambivalences, the big decisions, the conflicts, the surprises. It captures and illuminates a significant time so that women like you can be released to recognize and validate their own feelings. There is a legitimate place for the mother of the groom who needs and wants more than a pat on the head and the classic advice to "Just wear beige and don't say anything."

I.

Your Son Is Engaged!

"WE'RE ENGAGED!" IT'S VERY EXCITING to hear those words tumbling off your son's lips. Other terms, like "going together" or "significant other," indicate a private relationship between them that excludes you and everyone else. "Engaged" is a big word, a familiar word, a word that includes you because you've been there and can see what's ahead for your son as the possibilities of his life expand.

Even though you have anticipated it, the word may still catch you with a surprising rush. It's a good thing that many engagements often evolve through various stages of commitment, intervals of time during which two people gradually come to see themselves as a couple. These intervals are just as important for the mother of the groom as she begins to understand this new "couplehood" and finds her way to establish a relationship with it.

Some Questions

This critical transitional time in your life is a time of ritual and ceremony that evokes, as it must, a heady emotional brew. Are you happy? Well, yes and no. You have fears and hopes—most of which you feel too insecure or self-conscious to share. Will your son's bride like you? Will she be your friend? Will your relationship be a mother-daughter thing, or a mother-in-law slash daughter-in-law thing? Will your son, whom you have nourished, nurtured, and loved for all these years, continue to include you in his life?

The Past As Prelude to the Future

You begin to look ahead with a sense of apprehension, anticipating the future with a certain amount of fear and trepidation. What will happen to you? What will be your role in this new relationship? How will you be included in your son's life?

When Nan, whose son had recently married, was asked how he was doing, she answered, "We lost him." No, he hadn't died, but she felt as if she had lost her son. She felt hurt that her daughter-in-law's family had simply "taken him over." Because Nan didn't take the steps to bond with her daughter-in-law or her family, she now hears from him only occasionally, on her birthday or on some holiday.

Will you also become anterior to your son's life, or will you be included as part of a larger family? Will there be a rivalry for your son's affection, as in the story line of so many plays and novels? Will you gradually become inconsequential in his life? Or will you feel as though you've lost your son and be haunted by that old saying that "Sons always go with the girl's family"?

The answer is no.

Just go back and remember those other times when you and your son separated, possibly when he went off to college or got a job in another city. He came home on holidays or birthdays and filled you in on his new adventures. He told you about his friends and his work, and your life became richer as you added his new life to yours. You had little bits of "together" with lots of space in between so that both of you could gradually learn to accommodate that sense of separation. Now, with his forthcoming marriage, you can do the same thing, becoming a part of his new life as his new stories reach out to you and become a part of your life.

If You Know Her, If You Don't

If your son is marrying the girl he has been dating since high school, you have had time to get used to the idea of his marrying her and separating from you. But if your son is off at college, for instance, he may surprise you one day by asking if he can bring someone home with him when he's coming in next week—a girl he's been going out with. Of course he can. And he does, and gradually over the next few months she comes home with him often, for barbecues and birthday parties. You begin to learn all about her and her family, her career plans, and particularly all the plans she and your son are making for the future. No question, they are going to get married. You quickly absorb the idea and hope they wait until they at least graduate or until one of them gets a job.

Let us fast forward a few years and look at another situation. Your son has waited many years after graduation and has reached a marriageable age without being connected to any one woman. You often find yourself curious about the women he dates, and you begin to hope that he will find someone soon— possibly just like you. Once my son showed me a picture from a party, and I saw him with a pretty dark-haired girl. Ah, yes, he liked her very much, but she left him for a boyfriend in Paris. Unbelievable! How could any woman reject such a handsome, intelligent, kind, and loving young man!

As your son gets older and still remains unattached, you may have to deal with friends who ask you often how your son is. Translated, you know this means, "Is he going with anyone?"

You genuinely want him to go with someone, not just to satisfy inquisitive friends but for his sake. Mothers have exactly the same wishes for their sons as for their daughters. You want your son to be happy in love and to sustain and nurture that love into marriage. Contrary to the popular image our society often projects of the threatened, clutching woman whose son is being taken away from her, or the mother who reluctantly donates her prince to an unworthy other family, mothers want their sons to find love and to be loved. You hope only that you have prepared your son adequately.

Now, with his engagement and forthcoming marriage, whatever relationship you have had with your son should prevail. It should grow and be enriched as he develops this new life with the woman he loves, a woman who is going to become an integral part of your new life with him.

Let's Get Rid of the Baggage

Unfortunately, an unpleasant aura has always permeated the words "mother of the groom." And that's not even half as bad as "mother-in-law." Only the French have a nice word for her: *la belle mere,* which means "the beautiful mother." In our culture, she is portrayed as either wickedly possessive or, most often, part of a comic routine. We're all too familiar with the jokes. Humor has its own way of telling us the truth. We often make fun of those things we are afraid of, the better to cope with them.

Did You Know?
The Navajo mother-in-law basket has a bell on it to let her daughter-in-law know that she is approaching.

"A Son Is a Son Till He Takes Him a Wife"

Joe and his fiancée, Gloria, had gone skiing and stopped on a hillside to admire the beauty of the snow. Joe called her attention to a red barn tucked in the far woods and remarked quite casually that his mother would love to see this sight. Gloria then turned to him and asked why he had brought his mother into the scene, implying that obviously he had Oedipal problems to resolve. Disturbed by what she said, in a moment of confidence, he told the story to his mother. While it was a comforting thought for her to know that her son had thought of sharing that moment with her, she was also devastated by his fiancée's response.

As a future mother-in-law, it's important to stop and remember that the woman your son is marrying doesn't know you yet. She may be afraid of you and of the hold you have on your son.

Looking Through Her Eyes

Take a moment to think about your future daughter-in-law. Consider that just as you fear that she will take your son away from you, she is afraid of the ties that have bound you and your son together, ties that could corrupt or inhibit the new and vulnerable relationship that she and her soon-to-be-husband are trying to form. She worries that you may be a hidden power, a threat to her happiness. You were, after all, very important in your son's life before his future bride appeared.

As the woman with a great deal of past influence, you now realize that you will be sharing your power with your daughter-in-law. She might think that it's better to keep you at a distance or to diminish you bit by bit. That's how the comics do it—joke by joke. As your anxiety about this new situation in your life creeps in, you might be asking yourself whether your invisibility at the wedding is only the beginning.

Consider This

"A man loves his sweetheart the most, his wife the best, but his mother the longest."—Irish proverb

Simple Questions, Complicated Answers

From that first phone call, when your son tells you about the special woman he just had lunch with, to your parting wave as the couple speeds off on their honeymoon, you will find yourself caught up in a whirlwind of complicated emotions, a curious mix of joy and apprehension. Here are just a few of the thousands of questions that may race through your head:

- Who is this new woman in your son's life (and now in yours)?
- What is she really like, and how will she respond to you?
- Will she enrich your relationship with your son or separate you from him?
- Will she call you "Mother"?
- Where will they be married?
- Where will they live?
- Does she have the same religious background as your family?
- Do religious differences matter to you?

- What is her family like?
- How does her family feel about the engagement?
- What will you wear?

The Question of Religion

Is it really important to marry someone from the same religious background? Some say, "Yes, of course, your religion is a part of your life." According to others, differences in religion don't matter as long as the two people respect each others' views. Madison, a devout believer, felt that living with two religions side by side made life richer and was good for the children, especially if the parents practiced their religions. Some people disagree and claim that the children always go with the mother's religion.

My neighbor Alexis, who is Catholic, was very upset that her son was marrying a woman who not only was not Catholic but who had also been divorced: "I can't do anything about it, but I'm not happy." She was sure her son and his future wife would run into many problems, especially if they had children. She consoled herself by saying, "Maybe she'll convert."

How Does Family Background Affect You?

Should her family's lifestyle, politics, or income influence your feelings about her?

"No," says Molly, a dental technician, who liked the girl her son was going to marry very much. "I'm not going to let her family influence my affections and respect for her. She is so sweet and bright and wholesome, but she comes from a crazy mixed-up home. Her parents are divorced. They are both artists, and each one is living with a lover. I'm not going to judge my future daughter-in-law by the way her parents live."

But Gwen, a pediatrician whose son was just graduating from medical school, says, "Yes." Her son was engaged to a girl whose mother was a recovering alcoholic and whose father had disappeared many years ago to live in the mountains of Idaho. She was genuinely worried that his fiancée's background would jeopardize their marriage.

On the other hand, Allyson's son Brad was marrying a woman whose father was a cardiologist and whose mother was a corporate lawyer. Allyson was very proud of the gene pool her family was about to tap into.

It's not easy to be the child of an alcoholic, but neither is it a tribute to your son's fiancée that her parents are successful professionals. Children grow up knowing much more about their parents than we often give them credit for. They know us for our strengths and weaknesses. And they make their own life decisions as they shape themselves within their own environments and opportunities. Children are not clones of their parents. They may or may not accept their parents' values. Genes are inherited, but behaviors are not.

As you get to meet and know her family, you will learn many things about them. It's more important to be learning about your future daughter-in-law, who she is and how in her own unique way she responds to life—and especially to your son. It's the chemistry between those two that matters most.

You'll Feel Better When You Talk about the Wedding

Talking to friends, especially those who are mothers of grooms themselves, will help you open up and explore the tangle of feelings you're experiencing. As you talk, you will sense your common needs. It's important to know that you're not the only one having these feelings. You will smile with recognition at someone else's confession, sometimes with guilt but always with relief that someone else has shared your same response— and actually had the nerve to express it.

At the same time, always remember that someone else's solution may not be yours. You know the facts of your particular situation; you must have confidence in your way of dealing with them. The important thing is to listen and not be afraid of your own feelings. You know you want to be a part of your son's wedding and of his future because he is so much a part of your life. The question is, what is the best way for *you* to become involved in what has to be one of the most precious occasions in your life? And where is the structure to let you in?

2.

Meeting Your Future
Daughter-in-Law

You look at the woman your son has chosen to be his wife and to be your daughter-in-law. More than anything, you want to have a good relationship with this new person in your life. "Engaged" is a time for kissing and hugging and saying "Wonderful!" In the midst of all that celebrating, how can the two of you come together? You may like her, but you may not know her very well, if at all. So what can you say to her? What can you do with her so that you two can get to know and enjoy each other?

Picking Up on Signals

The relationship with your future daughter-in-law has begun before you meet her. This indirect interaction could happen on the telephone, probably through your son. Maybe it began the day you didn't quite recognize him because his opinions, thoughts, and feelings sounded so different from the son you thought you knew. He used to love living in Vermont, but now it's "too provincial." The winters are too long, the spring too muddy. "Of course," you suddenly realize. "He's engaged, and someone else is influencing him."

Although you are happy about this new circumstance, the change can be a little disconcerting. You're not quite sure where your son is coming from, and you might find yourself analyzing his answers and becoming uneasy about your own. Be careful not to "think too precisely on the event," as Hamlet would say; otherwise, you will keep asking yourself unanswerable questions like, "What did he mean by that?"

On the other hand, one woman told me that she was relieved when her son became engaged because now there would always be someone to listen to him talk about personal, deep, and important things. She was glad that he would be supported forever.

What Is She Learning About Me?

You know that in the most natural and perfect way he is sharing everything with her—probably including many stories about you and your family. She is learning about you long before she ever meets you, and you wonder how you are being translated by your son. Is he telling her the *truth*? It doesn't really matter because it's his perception of you that counts. And that's what she is hearing. To make that situation a little more complicated, you also know that communication is a six-lane highway. The information he passes on to her goes through yet another transformation as it gets screened through her life experiences, values, and judgments. Not to worry. In time you will learn what her image of you is, and you will learn how to deal with it, polish it, or correct it, if need be.

What Am I Learning About Her?

In your telephone conversations or visits with your son, you are also learning about her. You might hear about how they met, where they go, where she lives, her last name (a quick clue to nation of origin), and her work. It's a really grownup time in your son's life; he can decide whom he wants to marry without checking it out with you first.

Yes, it's all right to ask questions—provided you use your common sense and don't invade his privacy. Don't ask about age or previous experience. Let him tell you what he wants you to know. This is a time to listen to what he says with interest rather than with the age-old need to judge, influence, and decide what's right for him. You will have time to learn about this new person whom you have not yet met. This is not the moment for twenty questions.

If you listen carefully, you will also hear things that he may not be telling you directly but that are worth your attention.

Maybe he mentions a book that he's reading or a trip that they're taking or a chocolate cake that she made. She is influencing not only his opinions but his tastes, his attitudes, and his habits.

Claudia had forever tried to enrich her son's life as he was growing up. When he was a little boy, she took him to the opera, to museums, and to the theater. "We always went to concerts on Sundays in one of those beautiful churches in New York. And we were readers. We didn't watch television; we read books." But none of it seemed to take. "He couldn't care less. He hardly ever read a book on his own—only what the English teacher assigned. We even gave him books for Christmas. But you know how they grow—always in opposition to you."

Claudia's ears perked up when her son, recently engaged, called to tell her they would be late for dinner because he and Nikki, his fiancée, were going to an exhibit at the art museum. "I was so happy; I couldn't care less about dinner. Here was a woman able to do in three months what I couldn't do in twenty-eight years."

The woman your son is marrying brings with her a whole other world. It may be a rich and wonderful world. She may be building on what you started, but she may also be introducing him to worlds he has never known about before.

Do First Impressions Matter?

Monica, who has just one son, told me that she knew the young woman her son brought home would be the perfect wife for him because the girl's name was the same as Monica's mother: Dorothy. That made for a wonderful first meeting because on the slightest evidence, Monica was prepared to accept the young woman.

However, it doesn't always work that way. Some first meetings are planned; others are spontaneous. Some are warm, while others may be cold or embarrassing. The occasion is not always one you can control, but whether you survive it is up to you. Just remember that you are not the only one filled with expectations and fears; imagine what's going on in your future daughter-in-law's heart. And in your son's.

Evelyn, a dietitian and mother of three sons, said that she had gotten tired of cooking for the various young women her youngest son, Eddie, always invited to dinner. So she was totally blasé when Eddie told her he was bringing a new girlfriend to meet her.

Enter Jennifer with a box of Godiva chocolates. Evelyn, who had intended to go shopping that afternoon, had an empty refrigerator and nothing to offer Jennifer but a glass of water. As a woman whose life's work involved food, she was mortified. But by the time Jennifer and Eddie became engaged, Evelyn had prepared them many wonderful dinners and demonstrated not only her basic generosity, but her culinary skills as well. That first meeting became a funny family story.

Although Angela knew that her son was going with someone named Alysse, she first met her future daughter-in-law without warning. Her son Danny stopped by the house at midnight on his way from Boston to New Jersey, where he was going to spend the weekend with Alysse and her family. When Angela heard the doorbell, she ran downstairs groggy-eyed in her old pink bathrobe. After a deep breath she recovered and greeted her son. Of course Danny and Alysse must stay the night. No, they didn't want tea or cookies; they were too tired. So Angela quickly made up their bed and tried to go to sleep herself. It was a hard first meeting and not the one she had hoped for. She had wanted to look beautiful and be bright for her future daughter-in-law. She assured herself that things would look better in the morning. Certainly *she* would. And she vowed to get rid of that bathrobe.

Wendy, a musician, twice married, now widowed, and mother of four children, had just moved into a new apartment. She called her son Barry to help her stack some shelves and generally help her to move in. With him he brought Marcy, someone she had never met. Wendy was annoyed because she had to empty boxes, sort out lots of paperwork, and tell Barry where to hang pictures and shelves. She had neither the patience nor the time to socialize with his new girlfriend. So she didn't. She never even offered her a cup of coffee.

Barry called her as soon as he got home and lashed into her for ignoring Marcy and making her feel so unwelcome. He and Marcy had become engaged, and, although he had come to help Wendy settle in, he had also come to introduce his fiancée.

Of course Wendy was embarrassed and apologetic. She even tried to put the blame on Barry for not telling her about Marcy. But the real problem lay with Wendy. When your son appears on the doorstep with a girlfriend, it's time to consider all possibilities. And simply as a matter of courtesy, Wendy should have reordered her priorities. Marcy and Wendy never did warm to each other, and Wendy spent many years estranged from her son.

Not knowing that you are about to meet the most important woman in your son's life can also be a blessing. Jane and Ron had just left a matinee in New York; they called their son Peter to join them for dinner. He asked if he could he bring his friend Renee, with whom he had spent the afternoon walking in Central Park. They knew he had been dating a Renee, and this seemed like a very pleasant way to meet her.

What they did *not* know was that their son, expecting their call, had deliberately made a date with Renee so that he could bring her along to meet his parents and announce their engagement. Neither Renee nor his parents had much time to build up their anxieties and expectations, which turned out to be a great way of doing things for everyone involved. You can't tell your son how to plan the perfect first meeting. You can, however, live in the moment and enjoy it with grace, sensitivity, and intelligence.

Two Parents, Two Responses

On their ride to meet Melissa, their son Evan's fiancée, Becky and Scott talked of nothing but their forthcoming meeting. They promised each other to act normal, to carry on a reasonable conversation with her without trying to dazzle her with their intellect and wit. Evan had been married before and had been deeply hurt by the divorce. "We wondered if we had been too supportive, too approving in the past and had inadvertently influenced his decision. This time we agreed to let Evan do most of the talking and not to offer advice when we were alone with him."

Becky saw how happy Evan was, how lovely Melissa was, how "great they looked together." The evening went smoothly, and the talk was bright and lively because they were all eager to please each other. "I saw my son watching us to catch our response. I watched myself stepping out of myself to listen, to observe and try not to judge as we talked about travel and movies and food. Two hours flew by.

"When my husband and I got back to the car, I swallowed hard and talked fast. I thought she was beautiful, friendly, witty, intelligent, loved all the things I loved. I was prepared to love her." Scott agreed that she was all of that, but still . . . he wasn't quite sure of his response. He would have to wait and see.

Here were two parents, mother and father, each responding in a classical pattern. Erich Fromm, a psychoanalyst and author of *The Art of Loving,* describes Mother as the subjective one, the nurturer, the protector of the child. Father is the objective principle in action, always preparing the child for the worst, the real world. While Father tries to find whatever flaw there is in Son's thinking so that he can correct it and lead him toward a better decision, Mother, on the other hand, finds the good and the positive and is optimistic that her son will ultimately make the correct decision. Father suffers with a sense of responsibility for always teaching his son the right thing to do; Mother tends to approve of whatever he does.

If you are married, your husband will certainly weigh in on this first meeting. It's best to recognize your roles in your son's life as you respond to his choice of a wife. You and your husband may differ in your responses, and it isn't necessary or wise to try to convince each other. As my husband said to me, "It doesn't matter what I like or what I want. I'm not the one who's marrying her. It's all about his needs and his wishes, his feelings, and his judgment about what will best satisfy him."

Choosing the Right Words for the First Meeting

Once upon a time, when seven out of ten people married people who lived within five miles of their own homes, it was easier to know the woman your son dated. More than likely you also knew her family. You probably had a long time to get to know your son's fiancée, with many opportunities to build up a relationship on small talk about likes and dislikes.

Today, however, distance truly lends the relationship a sense of enchantment—or rather of mystery. Geography often separates us from our sons. Jobs take them to faraway places and keep them traveling. They go away to college, an initiation into adulthood. Their relationships grow exponentially and far away from you so that you may not meet the woman your son is marrying until after they have become engaged. You may even meet her for the first time the day of the wedding.

Maddy's son met a girl from Bologna when he was studying in London. The first chance Maddy had to talk to the woman was at the wedding, which was held in the bride's family home in Italy.

How do you start a conversation and establish a relationship with the woman your son is going to marry after they've become engaged? It's not so difficult if you stay as close to yourself as possible and don't try to find out everything about her or tell her everything about you in the first ten minutes. Here are a few openers you can improvise on:

- *Gracious:* "Thank you for making Jeff so happy. This is such a good day for all of us."
- *Humorous:* "It's so good to finally meet you. Jeff has probably told you all about me, and I've heard such wonderful things about you. Where can we have lunch and compare notes?"
- *Easy:* "Call me Jenny." And take it from there.
- *Small talk:* "This weather is awful!" "The trip went very smoothly!" "We're so excited to meet your family at the wedding."

Cassandra told me that her future in-laws made her feel "so incredibly comfortable" at that first meeting by not asking her any questions except how she liked the trip she had taken in order to meet them.

Sound is always better than silence. If you take the initiative, you will make everyone feel more comfortable. Don't try to memorize any lines. Let the situation dictate the conversation.

Just start with open and welcoming arms. Body language says a whole lot. Try not to make the conversation "important." And don't ask her to tell you all about herself. If distance continues to be a factor in your lives, then frequent short e-mails, phone calls, birthday cards, and holiday greetings will keep you in touch between visits.

Overcoming the Identity Crisis

Now that you two have met and begun talking, several other critical questions need to be answered fairly soon. You have to identify yourselves. What does she want you to call her? What do you want her to call you? What does she *want* to call you?

What Last Name Does She Want?

Suppose your future daughter-in-law wants to keep her last name. That should no longer be an issue. The past thirty or forty years have made us all question many of the things we used to accept as given. Not long ago, women were always identified by their husbands' name, so that we were all introduced as something like "Mr. and Mrs. Allan Graham." Now, it's much more common to see "Janet and Allan Graham" in a listing or address. The wife also has a name.

Many women who marry today want to keep the family name that has always identified them. Your future daughter-in-law may want to keep her name for professional or personal reasons—even though she is very happy to marry your son and be a part of your family. She and your son will decide what last name their children will have. These are decisions they will make, and you, very graciously, should accept. In Spanish countries, the woman's family name has always been an integral part of her married name and her identity.

Now What Do You Want Her to Call You?

Here is the woman who is going to be your daughter-in-law, whatever that strange hyphenated legal word means. It almost sounds like a bump you have to find ways of climbing over. And one of the first issues to get over is the inevitable question, "What does she call you?"

Maybe you won't have to deal with it. Maybe she will automatically call you "Mother" or by your first name. In that case, she will have made the decision that is most comfortable for her, and it is best for you to abide by it. But if that doesn't happen, don't wait too long to help her out.

These issues are not insignificant; they can color a relationship. They can also help it develop. What are you looking for in a relationship with your future daughter-in-law, and how does what she calls you reflect that desire? What is she looking for in a relationship with you, and how does what she calls you reveal that? You are both at the beginning of getting to know each other.

Do you want a maternal relationship, one in which she calls you "Mother" or "Mom," a title that brings with it a certain aura of respect and even homage? Do you want her to call you by your first name and be your friend, establishing a light camaraderie between you? Will she call you "Mrs. Brown" and create a respectable distance between you forever? You don't want her to just smile at you and say "Hi," avoiding the issue completely. You want to give her a name she can call you as soon as possible so that you can talk to each other comfortably.

What Makes You Both Happy?

My mother was deeply hurt by the fact that my husband never called her "Mother." He was always respectful, but he never put himself in a situation that required him to call her by a name. He could not bring himself to call her by her first name—that seemed totally disrespectful, and calling her "Mother" made him very uncomfortable. So for my mother, it was always a "Hi" or a "Hello" and a smile.

Sara's son-in-law, who happens to live close to her and sees her frequently, calls her by her first name, but her new daughter-in-law, who lives in California and has only seen Sara twice, calls her "Mom," which makes Sara very happy. It satisfies both their needs.

Many mothers-in-law expect to be called "Mother" and even ask for it. Sandy told me how insulted she was when her future daughter-in-law, Janine, introduced her to her family at the engagement party as "Mrs. Grant." The day was saved when Sandy's older sister took Janine aside and quietly suggested that Sandy really wanted to be called "Mom" and that it would be very nice if Janine could manage to do it. Janine did.

Sometimes there are curious variations on the theme. Susan had accepted the fact that her future daughter-in-law,

Christina, did not want to call her "Mom," even though Susan had asked her to. She was, therefore, puzzled when she heard her future daughter-in-law call her "Mom" when her son was there in the room with them but call her "Susan" when she and her future daughter-in-law were alone. Maybe Christina was trying to please her future husband by calling Susan "Mom" when they were together, or maybe it felt like more of a family unit when there were three of them.

Another very curious and awkward situation exists in Donna's and Ben's relationship with each other's mother. Donna is a fundraiser. Ben is a reporter. Both are intelligent, articulate people, but both have stumbled over names.

Donna calls Ben's mother "Mother Taylor" to distinguish Ben's mother from her own, but the sound of it always makes Donna feel a bit like she were addressing a nun. Ben, also, has not yet found a comfortable way of addressing Donna's mother. Although he likes the woman very much and would like to talk to her, even on the telephone he has not yet found a name for her. He doesn't know what to say after "Hello." In a very serious way, he has lost out on a friendship because he hasn't been able to find a name for this nice woman who is the mother of his wife, and they have all been too embarrassed to talk about it.

In my own case, I was most comfortable asking my future daughter-in-law to call me by my first name. I offered the solution casually while we were on a shopping trip together. I could sense that the first-name option would be the best basis for a friendship with this mature and self-confident woman who was going to marry my son, and I didn't want to turn the topic into a dramatic moment. I did ask her, of course, if that would be all right with her. And she thanked me with obvious relief.

A Rose by Any Other Name

Discussing the issues is the only way to sort out everybody's feelings. Keep it easy and casual. If time has gone by, and your future daughter-in-law still doesn't have a name for you, you can bet that she has been thinking about it also and has probably been afraid to bring the subject up. She knows that the name game can be a volatile issue, and she's probably worrying about how to approach it. When you put it out there first, you clear the air and establish a precedent for solving problems.

Sticky problems with names will still pop up even after you think the situation has been resolved. What do you do when you send them a Christmas present or an anniversary card? Do you just sign "Mother" and "Dad," hoping she'll accept that without reading any subtext into it? As awkward as it looks on paper, my husband and I sign these cards with our first names (obviously meant for her), followed by a comma and then "Mother" and "Dad" (obviously meant for our son). Sometimes we just sign the card, "Love, Us."

Besides, more important than *what* she calls you is *if* she calls you just to talk. That's a happy moment, no matter what name she uses.

Building the Relationship

Here is this new person in your life, a very important person, someone you are eager to establish a good relationship with. How do these things happen? Well, you know what makes a relationship grow: doing things together, sharing stories, celebrating occasions, and time. You begin by finding occasions for getting together. If your future daughter-in-law lives close by, it's an easy and casual thing to do. Here are some ideas:

- Take her out to lunch.
- Invite her and your son to dinner. Don't make it a ritual occasion like every Friday night. But do it occasionally, and don't make a big deal out of it. If she's open to it, perhaps she can help prepare one of the dinners or make dessert.
- Go shopping with her.
- Spend a day at the art museum with her or go to a local craft fair. Look for opportunities to enjoy events together so that the two of you can be in the same room exchanging opinions, sharing ideas.
- Does she play bridge, golf, tennis? Do you? This is a natural and uncontrived opportunity to play together.

It doesn't matter if your son can't join you. In fact, it may be even nicer if just you and she can have the time together. The dynamics will be different when he is with you.

However, if your future daughter-in-law lives far away, you will have to do some planning. Invite her to your home for a visit—occasional weekends, birthday parties, Thanksgiving. You want to reach out to her, to find her, and not wait for her to find you.

The Visit and How to Prepare for It

No, you cannot redecorate the living room. You may have just enough time to buy a new pillow for the sofa. Plan ahead for meals so that you won't be frantically shopping or preparing food instead of enjoying her company as well as your son's. Of course, the occasion will dictate what the menus will be; a casual weekend is not the same as Thanksgiving.

On any visit, food is a big thing. Make a list of how many meals will be involved and what you will do for each one. Think breakfast, lunch, and dinner. You might eat one meal out, and probably, if it's an extended visit, they will want to go off on their own. Let them do it. That doesn't mean they don't like you.

Be prepared for all eventualities. Keep the meals simple and use your own favorite recipes. Find out what she likes, doesn't like, and is allergic to. Don't try anything new or anything that will occupy a lot of your time and energy (and make you anxious). Remember, you don't have to make everything to prove that you are a wonderful cook. There are also exceptionally good take-out foods in most supermarkets and local grocery stores. Do what you can ahead of time and put things in the freezer.

The dining-room table is one of the best places to get to know each other. Food is the universal solvent. Although there will be that undercurrent of something very important happening, focus on the food and the pleasure of sharing it with this new person in your life.

Where Do They Sleep?

After you've finished planning all the meals and shopping for them, the interesting question remains: Where do they sleep? Where do you put her luggage? Of course, you know they probably have been sleeping together at her place or his, but ask yourself: How do you feel about that arrangement at *your* place?

I remember years ago the passionate discussions I had with friends about who would sleep in what beds if our children brought home their girlfriends or boyfriends. We said things like, "Not in my house!" or "Send them to a motel!"

Even today, there are some strange dichotomies in some people's minds. Robert, an accountant, soft-spoken and conservative in politics but also a weekend motorcycle rider, totally accepted his son's sharing a bedroom with his girlfriend for the weekend. At the same time, he passionately forbade his younger daughter from sharing her bedroom with her boyfriend. "Yes," he said almost defiantly. "I believe in a double standard; it's okay for my son, not my daughter." Maybe that old chauvinist idea still floats around that the more sexual experience the son has, the more man he becomes; a daughter, on the other hand, should restrict herself and not bring too many experiences to the marriage, saving herself for the "prize" relationship with her husband.

Or maybe it's a question of how old your son and his future wife are. When my grownup son of thirty-four and his future bride of thirty-two appeared on our doorstep, we put all their luggage in the guest room.

The Giving of Gifts

My future daughter-in-law visited us on the weekend of her birthday. A present was called for. A *first* present. Giving a gift to your future daughter-in-law is one of those small but sensitive and carefully considered gestures. You don't have to wait for a birthday, however, to give her a gift. If she's a guest in your house, go ahead and put something on her bureau. If you're shopping for something you need, and you see something out of the corner of your eye that makes you think of her, buy it and give it to her. Gift giving is an inherently generous act. In ancient epic poems, the good guys are often identified as the "gift givers."

But what to give is sometimes perplexing. What is an appropriate gift to give at this point in her relationship to you? You're just getting to know her and aren't yet quite sure of her likes and dislikes or her taste in jewelry, clothing, or perfume.

Evelyn, a friend who is a really wonderful cook, gave her son's fiancée a pair of cooking tongs when they came for a visit. It may seem an odd gift, but it was a perfect one for her to give.

Cooking is a very important part of Evelyn's life and her work, and these tongs were her favorite kitchen tool. It was the most personal gift she could have given.

My husband thinks that if you buy a woman fancy soaps or lotions, you're implying that she needs a bath. He has, of course, begun to learn through his daughter-in-law's pleasure what bath extravaganzas every woman likes to have.

If you've listened to this young woman in your house, then you know what music and books she likes. If you've paid attention to the way she looks, you've noticed her clothes and the colors she likes to wear. Surely you can find a scarf, a sweater, a belt or, perhaps, a photo album—good for all those future pictures she will want to have. I gave Lisa a T-shirt on her first visit to our summer home in Martha's Vineyard, one decorated with lots of flowers and the words "Martha's Vineyard" weaving in and around them. I was comfortable giving it because it was simple, it was pretty, we had just come to know each other, and I hoped it would always remind her of that good time together.

And Her Family?

While you've been sharing your stories with her, be sure to ask about her family and get to know their names. Your son has probably met most of them, and their names are becoming familiar to you. That's a good thing. Build on it. Ask about her mother and her father, her brothers and sisters. Be pleased if they are reaching out to him just as you are reaching out to their daughter.

You will be curious about this other family your son is beginning to relate to, and in due time you will meet them. Ask for pictures. Take pictures of yourself and your family and send them on to hers. Just try not to be jealous of all the good times he may be having with her family. He may have found a new "best friend" in the girl he's going to marry, but he hasn't found a new and better mom in hers.

A Biblical Mother-in-Law Story

From the Old Testament, remember the tale of Ruth and Naomi, when Ruth says to her mother-in-law, "Whither thou goest, I will go" and "Thy people shall be my people."

What If Something Troubles You?

Suppose in those first few meetings, you haven't felt a reciprocal warmth. She hasn't responded to you as openly as you had hoped. You want so much to like her, but suppose you don't? What exactly is your role at this point in your son's life? Do you have any other responsibility than to support his decision? If he's eighteen, that's one thing, but what do you say when he's thirty-four, a grown man?

Sonya, a teacher and department head of physical education, advised, "Be honest! If you saw your son driving his car toward the edge of a cliff, wouldn't you shout, 'Stop!'"

Yes, but . . . can you really be totally honest with him about her, risking her anger forever if you don't exactly like her and she finds out what you've said (and she surely will)? Is he honestly asking for your opinion? Or do you tell him what you know he wants to hear? Is he still seeking your approval? Are you still seeking his? If you do have any qualifications or objections, is this your problem or his?

We parents can be an arrogant lot. Because we love our children so much, we mistakenly think we know all about them and what's best for them. Our wishes and longings and images are so mixed into the reality of our children that we often never recognize their private needs, what makes them different from us.

Then take it one step further. Suppose he listens to your superior wisdom and is sorry ever after or defies you in an act of self-assertion? You want more than anything to know if she is "good" for your son. Not "good enough," but *good*. You're not talking about preparing meals and ironing shirts. "Good" means good for him to grow with, to be with, to become his best self with.

So what do you do? Remember these are early impressions, responses that will probably change over time as both of you get to know each other, especially as your son helps that to happen. Your best response is to play the hand you have been given, thinking ahead and behaving sensitively and sensibly, always aware that your responses will shape the future of your relationship with her and with your son.

Three Women, Same Problem, Three Different Responses

Barbara was surprised by the tone of anger and sarcasm in the bride's voice on the morning of the wedding when Barbara asked her how everything was going. "We're managing quite well, thank you." Barbara had thought she was asking a nothing question, even a funny one because, "Everyone knows that the day before the wedding, everything goes wrong. Maybe she thought I was criticizing her family or her own ability to take care of things." Later the next day, however, at the wedding reception, her daughter-in-law found a moment to apologize, explaining that she had had an unhappy relationship with her own mother, that she was responding out of habit, and that it might take her a little time to trust a new one. Barbara was relieved and so glad that she had waited for an explanation and not followed up with an angry retort.

Lois was disappointed in the woman her son wanted to marry. She had hoped for a brighter and a prettier woman. When she met the girl's parents at their engagement party, she thought, "Oh well, the apple doesn't fall far from the tree." Of course, her future daughter-in-law sensed those feeling, and today, many years later, Lois regrets those early judgments and actions. What she didn't know at the time was that her future daughter-in-law had grown up in a very unloving family, the middle child of parents who rarely extended themselves to her. Today, in fact, her daughter-law has very little to do with her own family, and Lois is trying to make up for lost time so that she can enjoy her son and her grandchildren. "My daughter-in-law was very different from me," Lois said, "and I probably did not make the effort to bridge the difference. She was a nice woman; we didn't quarrel or anything like that. I didn't know that much about her, and I didn't bother to ask. But then we lived so far apart, it was not possible to have lunch, to see each other often enough to get to know each other better."

Feeling the loss today, Lois is trying to improve the relationship with more informal phone calls, not just on birthdays and Christmas, as well as frequent e-mails. "It's a work in progress," she says with a smile.

Rachel was surprised and not really pleased with her son's choice of a wife. Because Rachel's family was prosperous and because she thought her son was so handsome, Rachel expected him to bring home a beautiful and wealthy woman. Instead, he introduced his mother to Sheila, a shy young girl from a small town in upstate New York. Sheila came from a poor and broken family. Her mother had been forced to work all through Sheila's childhood. Rachel learned all of this and instinctively put her arms around Sheila. She knew that Sheila had missed out on having a mother's loving attention, and she literally reached out to her future daughter-in-law to provide her with that lost relationship.

Recognize the fact that the woman your son is marrying has her own history, her own way of responding to "Mother." You don't know what her family ties are really like, how vulnerable, how strong, how open, or how cautious she has learned to be about family. She is also not your daughter—nor is she your wish for a daughter, if you have none—and she's not your son in another form. She is a new person in your life, and she is also a grown woman.

So if this young woman your son has become engaged to isn't immediately what you had conjured up for him and for your own daughter-in-law, be patient with her and with yourself. Life has a lot more to teach you.

3.

Family Matters

Do we just marry each other, or do we marry families? Your son's marriage will give him another family. The way he responds to his wife's sisters and brothers, mother and father, uncles and aunts will be up to him, but the way his connections with them will affect you, and the way you will fit into this new family that comes along with the bride will give you many things to think about.

You are both eager and anxious to meet them. You're eager because they will be an important part of your son's life and anxious because you want them all to like you, and you earnestly hope you will like them. The prospect of getting another family, meeting a whole new cast of characters with people casually known as your "in-laws," is a big idea. Mostly you hope they are nice and friendly people.

Your son is probably not giving you too much information, and you don't want to ask probing questions, but how do you learn about them? How do you go about becoming a member of someone else's family? What's the best way to meet them? You're curious about their house and would like to see it. It would silently tell you all about them, about their personalities, values, hobbies, and tastes. What do they talk about? What don't they talk about?

A Wise Observation

"One would be in less danger / From the wiles of a stranger / If one's own kin and kith / Were more fun to be with."
—Ogden Nash

What Does Family Mean to You?

Families mean different things to different people. Some people like the idea of acquiring a new family, of adding new people to their lives. My mother thought it was the natural and logical way for families to grow. My husband, on the other hand, who was brought up by two angry parents, had very negative feelings about family and about being obligated to people he had no choice in selecting.

Is the need for family possibly a gender issue? Are families more important to the mother of the groom than they are to the father of the groom? Most women want families, want to build them, marry into them, and spend the better part of their lives maintaining them. Many men, however, seem to be either neutral about the idea or threatened by it. Perhaps they fear the possibility of losing the woman they married in the family she's eager to build. Some men even seem pleased when their grown children leave home. No empty-nest syndrome for them. They finally have their wives back again.

What Is a Family?

"Actually, family members are mirrors of every facet of your life. They know you better than anyone in the world and are willing to overlook and forget. They've seen you at your best and your worst. Often, they're colossal bores. They've told the same stories a hundred times, but sometimes the familiarity is like an old bathrobe, too old to brag about in public, but too good to discard yet. Like it or not, you're bound to them by your history."
—Erma Bombeck

You are not naïve. You grew up in a family, and you know that not everybody around that table at Thanksgiving is lovable. With all their flaws and problems, however, we hold on to families and look to them for comfort and help. Maybe we're put in families to learn about survival, revival, compromise, humility, separation, return, forgiveness, and ultimately, accepting—realizing that we could find fault with almost any group of people we would ever know so intimately. Possibly now with your son's marriage, you could meet the family you have always longed for, finding people who understand you, sympathize with you, and truly appreciate you. You could finally find your ideal family, or you could in many ways help to create one.

Why Is Her Family Important to You?

Don't worry about them, my cynical friend Laura told me. "You'll probably never see them again except at other weddings and funerals, so forget about them." Wait a minute! Not so fast.

They Helped to Shape Your Future Daughter-in-Law

In most situations, your future daughter-in-law's family is an important part of her life. Unless you know differently, you can assume that. The parents of the girl your son is marrying have provided the genes, the values, and the culture in which your son's future wife has grown up. They have helped to shape her attitude toward mothers and fathers, men and women, husbands and wives.

Your Son Will Be Spending Time with Them

You can also assume that your son will become involved with them. They will become an important part of his life because his wife will want to include them in many activities of their married life. Your son may very well be spending a good deal of time with them and enjoying their company. And you may have to process a whole new set of emotions as your son begins to accept another family as part of his new life.

Don't feel you are losing your son if he enjoys being with her family. Alice was almost ashamed of being jealous of her son's new relationship with his fiancée's family. "He was working in California and having Thanksgiving dinner with her family, while my husband and I ate at home in New Jersey. Like a good son, he called to wish us a happy holiday, and we tried not to look at the empty space at the table. He was having a great time and getting ready to go outside and play touch football with Olivia's brothers and sisters. I imagined the fun he was having while we sat home saying how nice it was just to be alone together but not really meaning it. I couldn't help comparing our home, the one Jimmy had grown up in, with the one he was now enjoying in California. Jimmy is our only child, and now here he was with her brothers and sisters and probably lots of cousins as well. He must have been in heaven."

It took Alice a little while to stop feeling left out of the fun and to stop feeling inadequate as a mother who had not been able to fill her son's needs. "I stopped weeping with self-pity and began acting like a grownup mom. We had given our son many satisfying and happy experiences, the best of what we had, and the values we had lived by. We had probably even made it possible for him to be comfortable in his new surroundings, to enjoy a whole other life, apart from ours."

Once Alice resolved her own insecurities, she was free not only to enjoy listening to her son's stories about how he liked being with Olivia's family but to reach out to the family that he was enjoying, the family that had become important to him. If this new family is important to your son's happiness, then it is important to yours.

And Then There Are the Grandchildren

There is another reason for you to develop a positive relationship with her family. These people, who are still strangers to you, will be the grandparents of the children your son and his wife may have. You will interact with them as you participate in the special events that will be part of your grandchildren's lives. As the "other" grandparents, they also will have special values and gifts to give to the new generation, and you will want to learn about them and respect what they have to offer.

For your sake, for your son's sake, and for the sake of grandchildren yet to come, you want to put forth your best efforts to create a happy and extended family.

What Do You Call Them?

There's a language glitch in referring to this new family. What do you call the people in your daughter-in-law's family? Do you refer to them as your son's in-laws? You can't really call them *your* in-laws because your in-laws would refer to your husband's family. Would your daughter-in-law's family then be "kith" or "kin"?

A name makes a thing special and different from other things. Take the Eskimos and their many words for *snow*—something very important in their lives. Other cultures and languages— Yiddish, for example—provide a vocabulary for the relationship by marriage of two families. *Machataynista* refers to your daughter-in-law's mother, *machitin* to her father, and *machatunim* means her father and mother and possibly all of her relatives. But the English language has no such words. Richard Mitchell, the "underground grammarian," tells us that if a language has no way of expressing something, then that thing does not exist for the people who speak the language.

In his Sunday *New York Times Magazine* column "On Language," William Safire calls this language omission a vocabugap (vo-CAB-you-gap), an example of an unfilled need in our English language. He cites the Yiddish word *mishpocheh,* "which lumps together just about everybody invited to the wedding."

It's interesting to wonder why the English language ignores the unique relationships between the two families newly joined through the marriage of their children. The phrase "in-laws" is a general term and, more accurately, describes the relationships the couple has now with their newly acquired sisters, brothers, mothers, and fathers, not the relationship their parents have with each other—as if the union of families is of no consequence. Maybe there is a hint of truth in what my friend Laura said. But even if our culture doesn't find the relationship between the two families important enough to be called anything, you should feel differently. If you want the relationship to be important, and if you believe it will add richness to all your lives, then as the mother of the groom, you have a significant role to play in creating this new relationship as well as a responsibility to help make it happen.

Make the First Phone Call

One of the first rules of etiquette to follow as the mother of the groom is to contact the bride's family. Whoever thought of this did you a great favor by providing you with a legitimate reason for getting in touch with your future daughter-in-law's family right away.

Assuming, of course, that the bride has already informed her family of her engagement, you can consider the most appropriate way to get in touch with them. A phone call works best for this situation. An e-mail is too impersonal; a letter is too complicated. And be honest—you're curious to hear her mother's or her father's voice. It's important to talk to people; the voice conveys so much more than the written word.

In addition, there are more fundamental reasons to get in touch the first time by phone. People feel awkward writing notes, especially to a stranger. And what do you say in such a note? Do you introduce your family? Do you begin making plans? Do you suggest meeting for dinner or visiting each other? And then there's the question of what you expect to happen as a result of your note. Do you wait for her to write one in return? Do you expect a phone call in return and then get hyper while you're waiting? Everything from tone to the right words to the spelling itself makes this a very complicated note to write. But on the phone, most of these issues never arise. You can hesitate or stutter; you can even speak in incomplete sentences.

The Meet-and-Greet

That first phone call will give you a perfect opportunity to move the relationship along. "When can we meet?" is the next logical question. Even if you can't decide right away on a date, you can start talking about the possibilities of meeting each other. By initiating the invitation, you are demonstrating to them (as well as to your son and future daughter-in-law) that you want to be a family.

A Get-Together at Your House

If it's possible, invite them to dinner. That way, everybody's seated and can talk to each other, and you're always more comfortable on your own turf. They get the chance to see you in your house surrounded by the things you value and that help to define you. Be assured, they are just as curious about your house as you are about theirs.

Consider these helpful suggestions for a successful dinner:

- Keep that first meeting as easy, friendly, and informal as possible.
- You may, but you don't have to, invite your son and your future daughter-in-law. Their presence will change the situation exponentially. If you would feel more relaxed with them to facilitate conversation, then by all means invite them. But being alone with her parents will give you all a better opportunity to learn about each other. Of course, you will talk about your children and the engagement, but you will also have more of an opportunity to talk about yourselves.
- Even though your brothers and sisters might want to come, keep the numbers limited and the preparation for the

dinner simple. You don't want to exhaust yourself. Save the big party for another time. Keeping the numbers down will make it much easier for you to talk to each other and will also give you probably the first opportunity to talk about the wedding plans. It's a way to become included from the start.

- Make a meal that you have made before. This is not the time to experiment or to try to knock them out with your culinary skills. You don't want her mother to feel that when she invites you to dinner, she won't be able to match what you've done.

- And remember the point of the occasion—to meet her parents, get to know them a little better, and ease the strangeness of a new relationship. Don't try to impress them with a resume of everything you have accomplished in your life. Be a good listener. Get them to talk. Remember, people enjoy talking about themselves.

Chelsea told me with great delight about the dinner she made for her future daughter-in-law's parents. Of course, she first asked if they had any food restrictions. Having none, Chelsea served cheeses, made her favorite chicken potpie, and baked apple crisp for dessert—all recipes she had perfected. "They loved it. We talked about the food, of course about the engagement, but also about lots of unimportant stuff. It was just a way to get to talk to each other. I learned that her father prefers Pimm's Cup to Scotch and that her mother loves those packaged chocolate cupcakes. I'll remember to bring her some when we visit them." You couldn't ask for a better getting-acquainted night than this one.

Also bear in mind that you want to create a situation that can be easily reciprocated, so that next time, in a few weeks, they will invite you to their house.

A Get-Together at Their House

They may beat you to the punch and invite you to their house first. That's fine, too. Of course you have to bring something, but don't ask them what you can bring to dinner. It puts the hostess in an awkward position. What is she supposed to say? When you visit them for the first time, be thoughtful and generous. Bring a gift. Unless you know what they like or need, bring a gift that appeals to you. It could also be something you made or baked. Just find something special—a good bottle of wine, if you know they like that, or some dessert you've either made or bought that is special. Find something you can give them to enjoy later, for themselves, not for this dinner. If you bring flowers, bring them in a container so that she doesn't have to stop everything and look for a vase. Time and good food will gradually help you to know each other.

A Get-Together at a Restaurant

Sometimes it's not possible or convenient to meet at your house. Also, you might prefer meeting them in a restaurant, a place you particularly like and want to share with them. You may find that more comfortable and conducive to easier conversation. After all, you don't have to get up and serve or clean up afterward. If you meet in a restaurant, it might be wise to invite your son and his betrothed because you are now in a more formal setting, different from your home. Just know that if you invite everybody to meet at a restaurant, you pay the bill.

What to Talk About

The easiest subject to talk about is your children, how wonderful they both are, how lucky you are that they found each other. But there are other subjects as well. If you're in their home, you can notice some of the objects in the room that interest you and get them to talk about the things they have collected and value. Also, what have you learned about them from your son and from their daughter? Tap into that reservoir of information. Is her mother a quilter? Does her father play golf? Avoid getting into partisan politics unless you absolutely know where these people stand—and you agree with them. Looking ahead, you can certainly begin talking about the wedding. Listen to where they are starting from, and make yourself open to their ideas and available to help with anything. Take the lead from them.

Where Families Are Concerned

"Better the worst horse from the best stable than the best horse from the worst stable."—Old European adage

Are Your Families Similar or Different?

You never know whether similarities or differences will bring families together. Similarities may but don't always bring people together. And differences in religion, social status, race, or nationality don't necessarily separate people. In many cases, they enrich and nourish the families involved.

Similar Backgrounds

It's easy to talk to people who come from the same background as yours. If you went to the same schools, read the same books, or have similar likes and dislikes, conversations can flow and build a relationship quickly. I know someone who has developed a closer friendship with her daughter-in-law's family than with her daughter-in-law. Both parents get together often because they enjoy each other's company. Their relationship also makes it easier for her to call her daughter-in-law and to plan social and holiday occasions that will include all of them.

Similarities in religion and in culture, however, don't necessarily guarantee a happy union. Carolyn's son, Harry, was engaged to Brianna, a very sweet and bright young woman. The families met for dinner in Brianna's house. Both families had the same religion and similar backgrounds. Everything should have worked to bring the families together, but the evening didn't go well. Conversation was difficult. Was it the combination of her silent parents, both dominated by a boisterous sister who seemed to be in charge of the family? The tension around the table grew throughout the evening, which ended shortly after dinner.

The fallout of the evening affected Harry and Brianna; both felt that something very deep and vital was working against them. Brianna, who was very close to—and protective of—her family, decided to break off the engagement. Harry did not object.

"Perhaps it was for the best," Carolyn said. Although she liked Brianna very much, she thought, "Maybe they didn't love each other enough, and they just used the differences between the families as an excuse." Perhaps Carolyn was right. When the couple saw the failure of their families to get along with each other, they might have examined their own relationship and found it not strong enough to continue.

Although you are an important character in the drama that is taking place, you need to realize that the couple is witnessing your response. Your son and his future bride are watching you and her family, looking for positive signs between you. It's important to them that you like each other. A good relationship between the families helps the couple to know that they have an extended family, a mutually accepting safety net of people who get along with each other and who also love them. You need to realize how very much the couple wants their parents to get along with each other, even to like each other.

Appreciating Differences

Ella met her future daughter-in-law's family on Christmas Eve, when she was invited to a Vigilia, the Polish Christmas

Eve dinner of traditional fishes. This would not have seemed extraordinary except that Ella was Jewish; at first, coming into this holiday family scene made her feel uneasy. Here was a Christmas tree with presents underneath it, gingerbread cookies with everyone's name on them hanging on the branches, snow falling outside, and a golden retriever chasing the children around the fireplace. It was a Norman Rockwell painting, totally alien to Ella's immigrant Eastern European background. Her son was marrying into a different world. How could she possibly fit into it?

"I had never been in a home like this. I grew up in an exclusively Jewish neighborhood in a big city. I didn't see a real Christmas tree until I was about ten years old, when some of my friends and I trooped over to a house three blocks away to look in someone's living room window with awe at the sight of the real thing. Now here I was, a guest in a totally different world from the one I lived in, a world my son was about to become a part of.

"I was so self-conscious that for a while I could only just smile and say how nice everything looked and how happy I was to meet everybody. But by the end of the evening, I really was. The dinner was delicious. We talked about many things, nothing serious. No heavy politics. Just small talk about family and work and childhood stories."

Despite the differences in background, the evening worked well for Ella. Social small talk about likes and dislikes really works to lubricate the wheels of conversation. Responses can lead to more responses.

As you talk to each other, you soon discover commonalities as well as differences, but differences need not be threatening. Differences can be fun; they can enrich the conversation. Ella and her future daughter-in-law's parents talked about the different worlds they had grown up in, mining memories that made them laugh. Here was Ella in an entirely different world from her own, sharing hers and learning about theirs and enjoying it.

Interracial and Cross-Cultural Couples

When the Katharine Hepburn/Spencer Tracy movie *Guess Who's Coming to Dinner* came out in 1967, we all wanted to embrace the handsome young Katharine Houghton and Sidney Poitier and certainly invite them to dinner. In real life, although we have become much more accustomed to seeing interracial couples, the effects of racism and strangeness have not entirely disappeared. These attitudes present their own special problems as couples and families seek to find common ground.

Bill and Janet are African Americans, and their son Patrick is marrying Nora, a white girl from Indiana. "Her parents came to meet us last week," Janet said, "to check us out." Bill added, "I think we passed, but the bride warned us that not everyone in her family may think so. Even though we have made it socially and economically, I don't know if we have made it racially." But Janet added, "I'm optimistic, and we'll do everything to make it work."

When Deborah's son, Rob, introduced his mother to Felice, a Filipino nurse, small and dark-skinned, his mother almost went into mourning. Deborah was white, from a prosperous farm family in Georgia. Deborah was barely polite to Felice. Privately, she told Rob, her only child, how sick she was over his choice. Although times have changed and cultures have learned to accept each other, for Deborah the union of different religions and races was still hard to absorb. It was okay for other people, but not for her.

As the mother of the groom, Deborah denied herself the pleasure of sharing her son's happiness. Felice and Rob made a very happy marriage, something Deborah could see, but at first only from a distance. It was when Rob told his mother that Felice was expecting a baby that Deborah woke up to the narrowness of her own feelings, to the love in her son's life, and to the possibilities of a grandchild, who might add laughter and joy to her own life.

Changes like Deborah's don't happen overnight. But if you love your son, with time and that love, your feelings can open up to accept what you once thought was impossible.

In our country especially, many families still carry the cultural baggage of skin color, eye shape, or some other similar stereotype. How can you help to overcome this heritage, to embrace the young woman your son has brought home to dinner who may be black, brown, or white, who may not even speak your language?

The first step is to get to know her so that you and she can be comfortable together and get over the differences. Invite your son and her to dinner, and make it often if she lives close enough. Talk just as you would with any woman in whom your son was interested. Ask her about her family. Does she have any pictures to share with you?

Don't be afraid to talk about race, about any issues that might trouble you. Your mutual concerns will come up sooner or later, depending on the amount of time you can be together and the friendship you can build. You can rightly assume that she is as much concerned about these issues as you are. And she will be relieved to know that you trust and respect her enough to talk about them with her.

Once you have established a level of trust with her, call her mother and invite her family to dinner—in your house. Here are a few suggestions for making the gathering a success:

- You might want to serve one of your favorite no-fail dishes, or you might want to experiment with something familiar to her family. Just to show them you care—and you can—if she's Brazilian, make a *feijoada* (pronounced *"fay-*zhwah-*dah*) and then everybody at the table can comment on how well you did it or suggest what you might do differently (not "better") next time. It's good for a lot of table talk, and it tells her family that you not only welcome them into *your* family but that you are willing to become a part of *their* family.

- If the languages are different, learn a few words in her language. Find out how to say "Hello," "Thank you," "Good night," or "That's okay." You can still have a good dinner together even if they don't speak very much English. With their daughter helping them, plenty of hand gestures, a few recognizable words, and lots of fine food, the dinner should go well and help you establish a positive relationship.

- Take pictures and exchange family pictures so that your relatives and their relatives can at least be able to identify each other before they meet.
- Take advantage of any family occasions to invite her and her family—birthdays, Thanksgiving, your niece's engagement party—so that people can have a chance to know each other socially, to begin to incorporate each other in their own private landscapes.
- Ask about any other cultural, family, or traditional customs they observe and would like to include in the wedding celebrations.

The word *wedding* itself implies bringing differences together. Your role in this wedding of differences—religious, racial, or cultural—is significant. When you care about the ceremony, the words of the service, the music, and the families, you help find your place in the lives of your son and future daughter-in-law. Beyond that, you can also expect to reap enormous personal benefits. You hear other sounds and voices and begin to understand how many different ways there are to open the same door. Helping to create the wedding may place a responsibility on you, sometimes a strange and uneasy one, but more often a rewarding one.

The Importance of Maintaining a Good Relationship

If the meeting has gone well, and you find yourself comfortably exchanging stories and ideas—actually liking these people—you can relax and count your blessings.

You could, however, also be working hard at the meeting, constantly adjusting your expectations as you listen to a perfectly nice other mother who has never read any of the books you mention and who responds to your stories about your love of cooking, for instance, with the pronouncement that she eats only frozen dinners because "you can buy anything you want." By the end of the evening, you should try to reconcile yourself to the new facts of your life. It's important to acknowledge that as you get to know people better, the facts may change. Although this may not seem to be the family you ideally would have liked your son to have married into, they are probably friendly and nice people. They may have many other virtues that will eventually come to light as you get to know them better.

And while you're learning about them, you can rest assured that they're also learning about you. More than just the stories of your life, they're finding out who you are, how you listen, what you respond to, and how. And if you really want them to learn about you, you have to be yourself. Don't be "on" for their benefit. Don't pretend.

Sometimes, however, you know from the beginning that you really have nothing in common with these new people. What do you do when your children are the only thing that ties you to each other? Don't minimize that tie. It's important enough that it might be all you need to honestly try to make the connection between her family and yours. It's easier if your future daughter-in-law has lived far from her family and has no particular feelings about needing to be with them. But if her family is close to her, both physically and emotionally, you have much to gain by establishing a good relationship.

Understand that there are degrees of disconnect and that these affect subsequent behavior. Even if you know that you will probably never be close friends with this new family, the alternatives are not disastrous. Often, the relationship simply has no place to go. "We don't dislike each other; we just have very little to say to each other. They're very nice people, but . . ." So be it. This allows for occasional holiday dinners together, a birthday celebration, a phone call from time to time to share some good news. This relationship is not unpleasant; the line, so to speak, isn't dead or broken. It just can't bear too much weight.

If the Relationship Is Rocky

We do not live in an ideal world, and though we cannot always create one, we need to try. There are no rules to creating perfect relationships. In each situation, the environment is unique, along with the parameters for what can and cannot be accomplished. Whatever the differences are—social, cultural, religious—you begin by wanting to connect with your *machatunim*.

Ways to Patch It Up

When Connie, a gentle, unsophisticated, heavy-set woman, walked into the lavish living room of her future daughter-in-law's family, she felt instantly that they had judged her and found her wanting. Connie felt that in growing up in this house, her future daughter-in-law had learned at her mother's knee to feel superior to people who were not slim, wealthy, or adroit at easy conversation. Connie is shy, self-conscious about her weight, and not a fighter. She found it impossible to bridge the social differences between this family and her own. For years, she has suffered silently, never extending herself for fear of being rejected.

Although we can sympathize with Connie, she had alternatives to choose from. Recognizing how much she wanted to be included in her son's life, Connie might have made an effort to call the girl's family. She could have invited them to dinner on a special occasion or asked them to join her for a movie, a visit to the art museum, or a speech at the local college. She needed to break through her defenses to have a richer life for herself and for her son. While she could continue to blame them, she really had herself to blame for a relationship that never blossomed.

If you have an unpleasant feeling after an evening with her parents—possibly a disagreement about one of the wedding plans or a difference of opinion as you moved into a controversial discussion—you have a choice. You can ignore the unpleasant feelings and continue as though nothing happened the night before, all the while remembering and nursing the incident, making it a story that you tell to friends. Or you can pick up the phone in a day or two and air the issue. It's not an argument; it's a conversation with someone in your family. That's not so hard to do, especially when you consider that it's much harder to let differences fester. It's amazing how responsible you can become for nurturing and maintaining this relationship.

You can also help your son during what may be a tense time for him by dispelling any of his unreasonable fears. "I think my son is nuts," Dana told me. He's afraid of marrying Crystal because her mother's legs are thick, and he thinks that's what Crystal is going to look like when she gets old." Dana told her son how foolish his fears were, how over the years anything can happen to either of them. He might lose his hair just as his father did. Would he want her to hold that against him? As the mother of the groom, Dana taught her son a very important lesson, helping him to overcome the superficial aspects of a person and hold on to what is really important between two people.

What If There Is No Hope?

Beth and her husband are lawyers. Their daughter had just gotten married, and they were still rejoicing in her happy union and in the splendid wedding they had given her. Beth was still feeling the glow of that wedding when her son announced that he, too, had found someone he wanted to marry. Beth was exuberant. She anticipated more joy to come. But early on, differences announced themselves.

"I thought it was really odd when Judy, my son's fiancée whom I adored, told me that her father could not possibly meet us for dinner to celebrate her engagement to our son. 'It was the tax season.' I was surprised because it was early in January. But he would not be free for lunch, breakfast, or dinner, not Saturday, not Sunday, not any day—morning, night, or noon until May. Finally, my daughter, who lived closer to their house than we did, made a special Sunday brunch to which he finally agreed to come after much pleading and cajoling from his wife and daughters.

"My daughter set up a beautiful table, the family silver, the china, the crystal, the whole nine yards. We brought bottles of champagne. Finally, they came, he and his wife—forty minutes late. We tried to overlook that. We also tried not to notice how cold and authoritarian he looked, the impression that he was here with us at great personal sacrifice. We thought to ease the tension with a champagne toast to the new couple. He wouldn't drink any of it, not even a sip for the toast to the new couple. He told us he doesn't drink during the tax season. He asked only for a glass of water. I have never met anybody like this in my whole life."

How do you pick up the pieces after that? How do you keep this relationship between you and her family from affecting your relationship to your future daughter-in-law?

To begin with, you don't have to tell her about all your misgivings. She knows. If she agrees with you about her family, then you have it easy. If not, you have to walk a diplomatic line. You don't want to involve your son, even though he knows, too.

It's never good to put him in the middle of a problem between you and your daughter-in-law's family. Again, if there's plenty of physical space between you and her family, that will pretty much settle the matter. But if her family lives close by, you will have to exercise some restraint and good judgment by managing to be pleasant whenever family events bring you together. This is not the best of all possible worlds, but it is the one you live in and the one you need to make the best of.

Some Guidelines to Follow

Remember, you can always be the positive agent whether the relationship between your family and her family is close or distant. There are always holidays to celebrate, birthdays to remember, and occasions to bring people together. Your role is to help make these things happen and to support this larger family structure—for your son, your future daughter-in-law, and the new family they may create.

Here are some important issues to remember:

- Set up an early meeting with your future daughter-in-law's family by calling them and by planning a get-together.
- Your future daughter-in-law's family is important to your son and consequently important to you.
- Believe in the importance of an extended family, and do everything you can to create one.

- Remember that differences in religion, race, and culture can be enriching.
- Remember that first impressions often change and that building a relationship is always a work in progress.
- Know that her family wants to know you as much as you want to know them. If you want them to know you, trust yourself to be yourself.

If you keep all of these points in mind, you're bound to have a relationship with your future daughter-in-law's family that suits everyone involved.

4.

The Holiday Spirit

JUST WHEN YOU THINK YOU'VE got this matter of family ties all figured out, a new dilemma presents itself. Thanksgiving happens, and everything changes. Holidays are family times, but now there are two families—yours and your future daughter-in-law's. Where will you spend the holiday? But more important, where will the soon-to-be-married couple go? And how will their choice affect you? What will happen to all the wonderful things you and your son used to do together on holidays and on special occasions? How can you best adjust your expectations and plans to include what is important to you, your son, and his future wife as well?

A Different Kind of Surprise on Christmas Morning

Christmas morning bloomed bright, clear, and cold for Phyllis and Jack, who were looking forward to the fun of gift giving this year because their future daughter-in-law, Audrey, was joining them. She came early, and there was much laughter and good talk as they exchanged books, sweaters, and jewelry. "And then, just when we were ready to serve breakfast, Audrey smiled at us and excused herself. She wanted to be with her family on Christmas morning. She would love to stay for breakfast, but she couldn't. So she left, and she took our son with her."

Of course, Phyllis could understand her future daughter-in-law's decision. She couldn't be angry, but she added, "I felt a hit inside, an empty feeling in my stomach as my husband and I cleaned up the dishes, folded the wrappings, and threw away the ribbons. I felt that my son had been taken away from me."

Changes Make Us Think

Although you know that change is in the air, there's a galactic distance between your intellectual understanding and your emotional acceptance of it. You never gave much thought to the complication that your son's forthcoming marriage brings, but it's one that will ask you to examine a new situation and adjust to a new set of rules. The holidays may be the first time that you realize things are changing in your life. Your son, who has often spent the holidays with you, may be with other people now doing other things. It is an illuminating moment when you see how important Thanksgiving, Christmas, New Year's, Easter, Passover, your annual Fourth of July barbecue—even Mother's Day—have become to you. Now as these special days all parade in front of you, you are compelled to examine them. It's important to see what is most important to you, to know how best to celebrate, and how to include the principal players.

You Have a Personal Investment in a Holiday

Over the years, you have spent much time, love, and energy to create the special ambience of each holiday. You created a special world for Christmas with a tree and lights, ribbons, cards, and decorations. For Halloween there were orange iced cupcakes; on the Fourth of July, you had flags and fireworks. You did this so that your son would have a feeling of joy and belonging to these celebrations, which would always remind him of his happy childhood and enrich him as an adult. Serendipitously, making the holiday special for him also enhanced your pleasure in it.

But now life is more complicated, and you are no longer completely in charge of how the holiday will be celebrated. You need to consider your future daughter-in-law's wishes, her family's customs and even how the future couple may choose to spend the holiday if they want to do something entirely different from either family's traditions.

Feelings Don't Change, Situations Do

Beverly is a pediatrician whose son recently graduated from medical school. Every Christmas Eve when her children were growing up, she and her son and daughter, Regina, would get together to read the Truman Capote story, "A Christmas Memory." They each took turns reading the story.

"It was always a beautiful and touching time," she says. "We looked forward to it each year." But last July, her son married, and he and wife moved to North Carolina. The following Christmas, it was not possible for them to be together on the holiday and to continue the tradition. "You have no idea," says Beverly, "how empty, how at a loss Regina and I felt. I almost called a neighbor to join us."

The Truman Capote story will always hold great beauty for Beverly. She can still share it with her daughter and a friend. Maybe one year, when her son and his wife live closer, they can join her once again. This is one Christmas tradition that can adjust easily to change and continue to give the participants pleasure and a sense of communion.

Practicing for Transition

It's surprising to realize how much emotion is invested in a Thanksgiving dinner, a Christmas morning, or any other ritual celebration—until that ritual changes or disappears. Ritual plays an important part in our lives because it gives us comfort. From these celebrations we take a sense of continuity and belonging, not just to our own family but to the larger community around us. Holidays provide a special time to celebrate the customs that have acquired meaning for us.

Unfortunately, holidays have become the province of the commercial world. Today, we all know we are being pumped up to expect more than any holiday can give us in terms of love and well-being and connecting. Everywhere you go, people are not only wishing you a happy holiday; they go on to ask you where you're going, whether you are doing the cooking, and whether your son is coming home for the holiday. Don't be surprised if you find yourself asking people the same questions. It's the expected conversation between strangers in the checkout line at the supermarket, where everyone seems to be competing in terms of how many people are coming to dinner, and success seems to be measured by the size of the turkey.

During your son's engagement, especially if it is a long one, you will have many opportunities to see what new conditions the holidays present to you. Remember that your son is also in a new situation, with new obligations and loyalties. Your son, his fiancée, her family, and your family are all coming at the holidays from different points of view. The important thing is to find the balance point without becoming demanding, turning into a complainer, or succumbing to disappointment. Don't be trapped in what used to be. Instead, talk it out together until what is lost in one place can be found in another.

Don't Be the Martyr

You don't want to be the mother-in-law who sits by the telephone and waits for her son to invite her to join them. Connie has spent half her life in this position. "I won't call them. Let them call me," is her answer whenever I've asked her whether she's going to Jeffrey's for the holiday. Each occasion raises the same anger, as she waits for Jeffrey and his wife to call her. They usually do, but not until she has spent her hours suffering.

Call them!

When something matters to you, call them. Ask about the holiday coming up, talk about it, and make yourself part of the planning. If you don't, you will just feed your sense of rejection, which will fester until you find yourself making speeches to yourself, to your son, and to his future wife at three o'clock in the morning.

Many Ways to Celebrate a Holiday

Listen to other people's stories and decisions. There's a world of possibilities out there for you to explore. Other people have been here before and have found their way:

- You can celebrate Christmas at your house and Thanksgiving at her parents' house. Next year, you can alternate the holidays.
- You can decide that your family will traditionally do Thanksgiving and her family will do Christmas, whichever holiday is more important to either one of you.
- If you live close to each other, you can have dinner at one house and dessert at the other.

- Again, if you live close to each other, you can share the same holiday: Christmas Eve with her family, and Christmas Day with yours. On the same lines, you can spend the first night of Passover with your family and the second night with hers.

- If you have you been concentrating only on how and where the couple will spend the holidays, enlarge your thinking and invite her family to enjoy the holiday in your house. Not only does this make for a bigger party, it's also a way to set up a family exchange plan for the holidays. This makes the celebration a cooperative venture, instead of a subtle rivalry for the presence of the young couple.

By taking the initiative and suggesting a way to share the holiday, you will avoid forcing your future daughter-in-law and your son to make a choice. Talk to them about the holidays. See what they want. Talk to her parents. It's a decision that you can no longer make alone. You also don't have to plan the whole future right away, just the holiday that's coming up. Everything in its own good time.

Partnering with Your Future Daughter-in-Law

If one of the holiday meals is going to be at your house, invite your future daughter-in-law to help you plan and even help prepare the meal. Bring her into your life by inviting her into your kitchen. Ask her to help you plan the meal first so that you can include some of her ideas and some of her recipes. Talk about appetizers and side dishes and entrees and desserts. Find out if she knows how to make a piecrust. If she'd like to learn, teach her. Tell her about some of your son's favorite dishes, and ask her if she'd like to prepare one. You'll help her.

By doing something together, in the most natural way, you can learn to appreciate and respect each other.

Divorce Can Complicate Matters

Whether either you or your future daughter-in-law's parents are divorced, you may have to consider another family in the holiday mix. This is especially likely if your son or your future daughter-in-law has a good relationship with the parent who is no longer in the family circle. You don't want to put your son and his future wife in the uncomfortable position of having to eat two Thanksgiving dinners—one at your house and one the next day at your ex's. If you're the one who is divorced, and you're on friendly terms with your ex-husband, you can always invite him (with his new family, of course, if he has one) to your house for the holiday. If you would rather not, then you need to negotiate a satisfactory arrangement with all interested parties.

Lots of feelings are involved, and holidays should not be the occasion for a power play of affections. Your son's decision to go to one parent's house for Thanksgiving, rather than to another, doesn't mean he loves one parent more than another.

The holiday celebration is not about the testing of relation-ships. By being a reasonable parent with everyone's welfare in mind, your attitude and your actions can make the day what it should be.

All Options Are Open

If for one reason or another you can't celebrate a holiday with your son and his fiancée, you are open to a variety of other options. You might want to travel, meet with friends, invite the neighbors, or give a party. Just because you will not be celebrating as you used to, the holidays needn't be a total loss. You may even find yourself celebrating different holidays. If the Fourth of July is important to your son and his fiancée, it may become just as important to you as Thanksgiving.

Jennifer had never celebrated Mother's Day. "I thought it was just a good marketing day for the greeting card compa-nies . . . until my son's fiancée told me that she thought it was one of the most important holidays in the year. She always either made brunch or dinner for her mother or took her out. Mother's Day was an occasion with a present and a card and sometimes flowers." It was a new idea for Jennifer, who quickly adapted to it. Suddenly the holiday began to assume impor-tance for her. She felt she could no longer ignore it without in some way upsetting her future daughter-in-law. So Jennifer has decided to plan a joint celebration—breakfast or dinner or coffee and cake together. It seemed to her another way of bringing the families together and strengthening family ties. And as an added bonus, she also began to enjoy the holiday.

It's a time to let go of what you have known and to create something new. Change is an ordeal. You can expect to feel a resistance to change that will inflict a degree of pain as you move away from the familiar. But you will also discover new and happy ways to celebrate holidays.

Many decisions, again, depend on geography—how close your son lives to you and to her family. If her family lives on the East Coast, you live in Oregon, and your son and his future wife live in Chicago, they may decide to spend holidays with friends.

Know that each occasion will present its own set of circumstances. Your son might have to work on Thanksgiving, or the couple could be moving, with no time for celebrating Passover, Christmas, or the Fourth of July. If they have children, Christmas morning will be very different for you. It might be at their house, where the children will be opening presents from Santa Claus.

A Different Ritual

It wasn't Christmas. It wasn't Thanksgiving. Mimi was deeply hurt that her son Paul and his fiancée, Tina, would not commit to come for dinner every Friday night. It was really Tina; she would come any other night, or even some Friday nights, but she didn't want to come *every* Friday night. For Mimi, Friday night was a ritual that involved prayers and candle lighting and a traditional meal. She had done this in her parents' home, every Friday night, and all her friends' married children did the same thing.

Mimi said, "At first I was devastated. I couldn't understand my son or my daughter-in-law's objections. This was a family ritual that brought us together every week."

Watch out for those rituals that you feel "must" be followed—whether it's dinner on Friday night or supper on Sunday afternoon. Remember that it's getting together that matters. Friday night or Sunday afternoon gatherings probably haven't been a part of your future daughter-in-law's life. You can certainly invite her to join you on those occasions, but don't make it a command appearance. Think how much happier you would be if your son and his future wife, freed from obligation, decided on their own to come for dinner on Thursday or breakfast on Saturday.

Mimi got over her disappointment a few weeks later, when her son and his future bride invited her to join them for pizza one Saturday night. She was delighted to accept. Her pleasure came from the spontaneous invitation, which was obviously made out of the desire, rather than the obligation, to be together.

HOW TO HAVE A "HAPPY HOLIDAY"

- It is important to take direction from the circumstances of your respective lives, not from the past or from images of what you think should be.

- It is equally important that you move positively into the true spirit of the holiday, rather than assuming a passive role and waiting to be asked.
- Realize that sharing the decisions with all the parties involved will make the holidays richer and better for you.
- Realize that your son's marriage marks a time for you to move on, to discover change, and to find a new pleasure in the change.

5.

Searching for Common Ground in the Details of the Wedding

THE WOMAN YOUR SON WANTS to marry may very well have been brought up in a different religious faith from yours. Different religious convictions will raise many practical questions and logistical problems, and you will find yourself involved in a whirl of new considerations. Who will officiate? If it's an interfaith marriage, what ceremonies will be involved? Where will the wedding take place?

The answers to these questions will bring a host of feelings to the surface, some declared and some previously hidden. Be prepared to inspect your own beliefs. Resist the pressures of family and friends pulling you in all directions, and ask yourself what is most important to you. Is it all about what you have been taught or what you really believe? Should you raise your questions and concerns now, before your son and his future wife have a chance to talk about their beliefs and the ceremony they want?

In general, it is better to wait and see what they decide. They are building their wedding and their future lives. You will have many opportunities to help, advise, question, ignore, accept, and also to look for meaning and satisfaction in the rituals that will involve you as well as your son and his future wife.

Type of Ceremony

Different options arise with same-faith couples as well as couples of different faiths. Instead of a ceremony that reflects their particular religious backgrounds, they may create one that reflects themselves as individuals—religious or secular.

Religious

If your son and his fiancée share the same faith and want a religious ceremony, they will choose the church or temple in which they wish to be married as well as the clergyman whom they wish to perform the ceremony. In some situations, you might be able to help them find the right clergy. Because the wedding was going to take place in the groom's hometown, while the couple lived in a different part of the country, one mother of the groom called around to create a list of three or four possible ministers who might marry her son and his fiancée. The mother then gave the list to her son and future daughter-law so they could make the necessary calls. The groom's mother understood that the couple needed to make the contact and the choice that would satisfy them.

A Secular Service

The couple may choose not to make their commitment in a religious context and may opt instead to be married by a judge, a justice of the peace, or even a layman with this legal power. You may feel differently, but this decision is theirs. Your role is to bear good witness to the ceremony, which can still be beautiful and significant. Secular services are often written by the bride and groom and can include poetic passages as well as testimonials from friends and loved ones. Such services can be held in many different kinds of locations, from a judge's antechamber to the ballroom of a hotel.

Even if the service is not exactly what you would have liked, you can still experience the joy and sanctity of the occasion.

Charlotte is a nominal Catholic whose son Edward was getting married. In her words, he was a "wayward" Catholic, and his bride was a nonbeliever. The wedding was to be held in a hotel ballroom. The couple had agreed to a secular service conducted by a judge. Although Charlotte understood all the logic behind their decision, she had secretly longed for something spiritual and powerful to consecrate her son's marriage. Not a religious woman, she still admitted to feeling sorry that her son couldn't be married in a religious setting.

The service included nondenominational passages from the Bible as well as readings that the bride and groom had selected. Before asking the couple to repeat the wedding vows, the judge paused and addressed the guests as well as the bridal couple. He said that although the service was secular, the bride and groom should understand that the vows they were taking were holy and binding and represented their deepest commitment to each other. "I can't tell you how happy it made me feel to hear him say that," Charlotte said. "And when they recited their vows, the words made me cry."

An Interfaith Wedding

"I want God at my wedding." That's what my future daughter-in-law said to me as she and my son began to make their wedding plans. But when one member of the couple is Jewish, the other is a Congregationalist, and neither practices his or her religion except for celebrating holidays, that invitation to God is both vague and complicated.

Today, this situation is not untypical. Many people who have grown up in a modern multicultural society only feel the need for a religious moment when they come to a significant occasion in their lives. Then they suddenly look for a church or call a rabbi.

If the interfaith couple wants a religious ceremony, and they cannot find the right person to marry them, you might suggest having two clergymen. Many interfaith ceremonies are performed this way. The clergymen share the wedding service, satisfying both sets of parents. Or you can make variations on this theme. One bride and groom, for instance, were married in church on a Saturday morning, had a rabbi repeat the ceremony that evening, and followed everything up with a reception that night. Everybody was happy.

It's sometimes hard to find a clergyman who will perform an interfaith marriage. Priests and often rabbis will not officiate at interfaith marriages unless the couple agrees to conversion or promises a specific religious education for the children. If your son is involved in an interfaith engagement, the subject of conversion will probably come up. It is best for you not to press the issue. This is a question best left to time and to the couple, who can answer it when they are ready. Several people I know who converted did so many years after their marriage.

Of course, it's always easier on your family if your future daughter-in-law wants to convert to your religion. Your son's decision to convert to hers, however, should not be a time of wailing and gnashing of teeth. People who decide to convert to their spouse's religion usually do it for a variety of personal and positive reasons. For one, they may really have become interested in their spouse's religion. The new religion may be offering them something that their old beliefs and traditions lacked. They may do it because they feel that their children will benefit from having both parents practicing the same religion.

In any event, conversion requires a great deal of thought and study. It is not something a person takes on casually. So believe that if your son decides to convert, it is because he has thought a great deal about it. This doesn't mean you can't talk to him about it, but you also need to respect his feelings and to honor his decision.

Your son doesn't have to convert to his fiancée's religion, and she doesn't have to convert to yours. Conversion isn't the only way different faiths can live together. Shirley is an Episcopalian. She attends Sunday services, volunteers to do the altar flowers, and attends church board meetings when big issues are involved. Her husband, who considers himself Jewish though he rarely attends synagogue, picks her up after church. Their daughter was married in Shirley's church; their son, on the other hand, was married by a rabbi because his fiancée's family was Jewish. Shirley and her husband have found their own way to live with two different religions.

Different couples work out their differences when they respect and love each other. Vincent describes himself as "a devout atheist." But he never objected to Chris's wish to be married in church. People with different beliefs can bring out the best in each other—and in you, too, if you can listen to the best intentions of your children.

You may be satisfied with the religious arrangements your son and his bride have made at the time of the wedding, but you cannot know how you will feel in the future. Karen's Catholic son married a Jewish woman, and he agreed that their children would be brought up in his wife's religion. Karen was comfortable with their decision because she knew that her son and his future wife had discussed the issue and that he had agreed to do as his bride wished. Because her son had no problem with this decision, Karen thought she would have no problem with it either. Years later, however, when the grandchildren arrived, she felt differently.

We often give easy agreement to abstract ideas. It's the reality that we may have difficulty dealing with. Karen had never anticipated her future feelings. She hadn't realized how her son's decision about the religious upbringing of her grandchildren would affect her until she was actually faced with it.

Although Karen maintained a respect for and participated in the Jewish rituals her grandchildren observed over the years, she felt increasingly that she also wanted them to share Christmas with her. They found a solution. The family has artfully created a new holiday they call "Chrisnukkah," in which they gather around a Christmas tree strung with blue and white lights. They give presents and then light a Hanukkah menorah. Karen has learned that an interfaith marriage can be not only workable and good for the children, but good for her as well.

Be open to the possibilities of difference. Roberta, a practicing Catholic, was very disappointed that her son's interfaith marriage would not allow him to have a wedding mass. However, when she entered the church and the music began, she was overwhelmed and surprised by her response to it. Her son and her future daughter-in-law, a cellist, had filled the church with music—twenty musicians, all friends, who played Bach, Mozart, and Elgar. The music they loved had become her son's "mass," his way of touching God. Roberta heard it and felt it. She was overcome by all those beautiful trumpet calls and organ swells speaking to the deepest part of her in their own transcendent language, holier than words. She, too, had found another way of celebrating God. Sometimes you can learn from your children and take direction from them.

There may also be an element of the service itself that bothers you or puzzles you, as the breaking of a glass at the end of the traditional Jewish wedding service puzzled Anna, whose son was marrying a Jewish woman. The best man is supposed to wrap a thin glass (nowadays more often a light bulb) in a napkin and place it under the groom's heel. The groom then smashes it and kisses the bride while everybody shouts, "Mazel tov!" and applauds.

Anna had heard many reasons given for this custom. Some said it commemorates the destruction of the second temple in Jerusalem in A.D. 200. Others said that the ritual symbolized the truth that life isn't perfect, and in the midst of joy you must not forget sadness. Still others said the bride and groom would have as many years of happiness as there were shards of glass. None of this made any sense to Anna. Then she learned from a rabbinical scholar that this ritual dates from primitive times and symbolizes the breaking of the hymen, and she suddenly found this ritual offensive.

But when she suggested that her son eliminate the ritual, he objected. The only thing that worried him was that he was afraid the glass would slip under his heel and bolt across the room. He and his bride liked the idea of smashing the glass. So did the rabbi, who said, "So many years of tradition have gone into the act, why worry about the original meaning, which is lost in history. All that remains is a sense of joy. It's a finale. Besides, it makes a terrific sound to end on." His response made sense to Anna, and she was happy to go along with the tradition.

Understanding the elements of a service by discussing them with your son and future daughter-in-law and her family can be your basic lesson in sensitivity. You can talk as a family about the kind of service you want and the kinds of prayers you want to include. You can carefully read the traditional prayers together and discuss anything anyone might think would be exclusionary. As you talk, you become aware of words like "Our people" or "in Jesus's name." This is an important time to affirm your belief that a wedding is a family affair and that you don't want anybody to feel left out of the service.

Searching for the right ritual involves more than words. The wedding ceremony itself is all about drama. Arlene's Jewish son was marrying Eleanor's Methodist daughter. When Eleanor began a discussion of what flowers and greenery should be used to decorate the altar, Arlene explained that in a Jewish wedding, the bride and groom often stand under a canopy called a *huppa*.

The *huppa*, supported by four white poles and covered by a religious cloth or by flowers, is set up in the area where the ceremony takes place. The bride and groom stand under the *huppa* throughout the ceremony. It represents their new home. Their parents and the other members of the wedding party may also stand under or around the *huppa*. That's what family life is all about, as parents, brothers and sisters, and close friends stand behind the new couple, ready to support and help them if needed.

Eleanor found the symbolic arrangement very appealing because it involved her and her family as well as the groom's family. She also liked the opportunity to be part of the service—quite different from sitting in the audience, observing the event.

An interfaith marriage can lead you to unexpected results as you find yourself often forced to reset the pieces of your own religious beliefs into a new mosaic. Jean's son Mark, a Baptist, married Isabelle, an Episcopalian who was at a time of spiritual transition in her life. Isabelle felt closer to Buddhist teachings than to those of her own church. The couple was married by a judge who included Buddhist, Baptist, and Episcopal rituals in the service. As a result of Mark and Isabelle's wedding service, Jean rethought many of her religious beliefs. Though she remained loyal to her own faith, she eventually joined a different congregation that was more open to her new beliefs about herself, God, and Christianity.

Where to Marry?

Probably the first question that will involve you, because it sets up the scene for almost everything that follows, is where the wedding will take place. Be open to all the ideas that will come floating toward you from the bride and groom.

House of Worship

A religious ceremony will probably happen in the church or temple of the clergyman who is officiating. Sensitive issues come into play when two faiths are involved. In her interfaith

wedding, Hanna wanted to be married in the interdenomina-
tional chapel at the private school she had attended because
it was a place of fond and personal memories and had no specific religious identification, a fact that pleased the groom's
mother.

Where to Hold the Reception

Many wedding ceremonies take place where the reception
is being held, often in a hotel or in a catering hall. The bride
and her family usually choose the wedding site. But Sally, the
mother of the groom, a generous and wealthy woman, offered
her home to each of her two sons when they married. One had
just started a business career, and the other had just graduated from college. Sally's home, set on a beautiful piece of land
surrounded by pines and maples and tulip trees, was a perfect
place to set up tents and have a wedding. The young couples
gratefully accepted.

Unusual Locations

Prepare to accept a variety of wedding sites. Today, a wedding ceremony can take place anywhere, not just in a temple,
church, home, judge's study, or catering hall, but on a beach
or in a garden, at an amusement park, or even in a converted
trolley-car barn, where one couple I know chose to marry.
Here's a word of caution about weddings on the beach: Make
sure the best man has a steady hand as he passes the wedding
rings to the bride and groom. I once heard about a mad search
for a ring that dropped in the sand. The minister, bride, and

groom all dropped to hands and knees and sifted sand through their fingers until they found the precious gold. And then there are the fabulous destination weddings held in places like Baja California, the Caribbean, or Martha's Vineyard.

A neighbor whose Catholic son was marrying a Protestant, and who was having trouble finding a priest and a church, threw up her hands and said she would be happy if they married in a tree house. She said it as a joke, but I'm sure the possibility exists.

Your Suggestions

Questions will come up along the way to the wedding that you will want to discuss with your son and his betrothed. How do you go about making suggestions, offering your thoughts graciously and sensitively, without looking like you're trying to take charge?

About the Location

In most cases, you will leave the choice of a location up to the couple. You may prefer a popular catering hall styled like the Chateau Frontenac to a loft in SoHo. But even if you are helping to finance this wedding, the decision about location is theirs to make.

Not all mothers of the groom have followed this advice. At lunch one afternoon, I overheard a young woman at the next table talking about her upcoming wedding. The soon-to-be-bride was practically in tears over the wedding site her future mother-in-law had chosen for them. "Paul and I just wanted a small wedding, and we picked this perfect little hotel on Long Island. But his parents are paying for the wedding, and they want all Paul's father's business associates to be invited, so they want us to have the wedding in Caracelle, which is a huge hall. It's just not my wedding anymore. It's theirs."

At a time like this, it's not simply a question of "he who holds the purse strings has the power." What's central is the wedding, which means that everyone involved must come together on important issues. It's about building relationships and listening to each other. You can be a part of the *conversation* about where the wedding might take place, but you cannot *decide* where it will take place.

About the Clergy

You may be surprised at the intensity of the feelings that bubble to the surface at a time like this. Maybe you haven't been a religious person all your life. Still, you might discover that at your son's wedding, you feel that you would like a priest, a rabbi, or the pastor whom you have known for years to officiate. The ceremony that's happening to your son is also happening in part to you; maybe, at this critical moment in your life, you need to see a familiar figure or hear familiar words to lead you through the passage. It's not inappropriate for you to make such a suggestion, along with your reasons for it, as long as you understand that the decision belongs to the bride and groom.

About the Ceremony

You may have a role to play in the search for an inclusive ritual. If this is an interfaith ceremony, find an opportunity to talk to your son and his fiancée about the service. What will you be hearing, observing, saying, participating in? And what will your family be witnessing? That way there won't be any uncomfortable surprises.

Religious ceremonies are important moments in our lives: baptism, confirmation, communion, bar mitzvah, and, of course, marriage. The ceremony tells everybody that a significant change is happening in all of their lives. Ceremonies help us celebrate the occasion or ease the passage from one step in life to the next. Beyond that, they also touch what is deeply familiar and connect us to the past, to a yearning for community and acceptance that might be subconscious until the moment arrives.

Don't hesitate to ask your son and his fiancée about the planning for the ceremony. The wedding ceremony is not just for the bride and groom; the ceremony is for everybody—family, friends, and neighbors. As the mother of the groom, you may be deeply affected by this ceremony, and you will want to understand it.

Sandra, who is Jewish, asked her future daughter-in-law to arrange a meeting for her with the Presbyterian minister who was going to perform the marriage so that she could learn more about the service. Everything he described pleased Sandra—until he asked her if he could include a reading from the New Testament about the wedding at Cana. He explained that although he was happy to include many Jewish rituals, as a Protestant minister, he would like to have a New Testament moment.

Consider This Parable

The wedding feast at Cana, described in John 21:11, is Jesus's first miracle; Jesus, a wedding guest, turns water into wine.

Because she was unfamiliar with the story, and because she feared that the mention of Jesus' name at her son's wedding might offend her relatives, Sandra was nervous about including it. She also knew that parables had interpretations, and she was uneasy about what this story might really mean.

Sandra called a good friend, a born-again Christian who taught Bible classes. According to the interpretation Sandra's friend found in a fundamentalist concordance, Judaism represented water, and Christianity represented wine. Judaism was deficient because it dealt only with the law, but Christianity was the wine because it brought God's love and mercy.

"I wanted to be ecumenical and fair, but I couldn't possibly accept this story and have it read at my son's wedding. I consulted with my future daughter-in-law, who suggested that I talk to the minister again and tell him what I learned and see what he said." Sandra said, "He listened, smiled patiently, and shook his head. He had never heard that interpretation. Where had I heard it? He talked to me about metaphor and how people read things into text that support their own beliefs.

Fundamentalists, he thought, would be likely to think in very basic terms of right and wrong, good and bad. But he didn't read the story that way. He liked the story of the wedding at Cana because he believed it was about the miracle of faith and love, which turns water into wine. And the fact that Christ's first miracle happened at a wedding is important because love and faith are the miracles that bring us close to each other and close to God. But if we didn't want him to tell the story, he wouldn't." Sandra, relieved and overjoyed, insisted he tell it.

Your Role in the Ceremony

Traditionally, weddings were ordained rituals with few opportunities for departure. But in today's weddings, there are many opportunities for you to participate. Besides creating a richer wedding ceremony, you can also become closer to each other, building the kind of trust that will help you to resolve other wedding worries more easily.

Doing a Reading

The practice of asking friends or relatives to join in the ceremony through readings has become increasingly popular. Today, almost every religious service includes readings, personally selected by members of the family or special friends. Whether they're original statements, selections from the Bible, or quotations from songs or poems, these readings allow people who are close to the couple to enter into the wedding. It is a dramatic and respected opportunity for you to actively participate in the ceremony.

Because a wedding is ultimately a family affair, it is perfectly acceptable for the mother of the groom to ask the couple how they would feel about her doing a reading at their wedding. If they haven't already thought about this idea, it might open up the possibility of including the participation of both families—another opportunity for everyone to become closer to each other.

Writing the Program

In one wedding I attended, the groom was French Canadian. Several family members delivered readings, both in English and French. The groom's mother translated all the readings and included versions in both languages in the programs.

Lighting a Candle

If there are candles on the altar, you can ask to light them. This will also give you a moment to say your favorite prayer, give a blessing, or make a brief statement to the bride and groom.

Music in the Ceremony

Music is an essential part of the ceremony, one where there might be room for your suggestions. The bride and groom may have their special favorites, and the organist will have a repertoire. But if a piece is particularly important to you, you can still suggest it. Most often, the suggestion will be welcome. Again, it's an offer that demonstrates your interest and your willingness to share what has given you pleasure. The prelude played while the wedding guests are gathering, the processional, the "Here Comes the Bride" moment, and the joyous recessional—these are just some of the musical moments that may give you an opportunity to suggest a piece. Remember, it's just a suggestion. Whatever makes the bride and groom happiest is what matters.

Music is always a personal choice. Laura asked about the music her son had chosen for his wedding service, so he invited his parents to hear the acoustic guitarist he and his wife had engaged to play at their wedding. Laura remembers standing on a street corner opposite an Italian restaurant in SoHo and listening to some lovely sounds wafted over the breeze. The guitarist was fine with her and her husband. She was a little surprised, however, the next day, when she heard what her son and his fiancée had asked the guitarist to play. The groom came down the aisle to the sounds of "Norwegian Wood," his favorite song, and the bride came down the aisle to "Feeling Groovy." People smiled and chuckled, including the mother of the groom. The wedding couple's choice of music made everybody feel welcome, happy, and young.

And then there was the simple Lutheran wedding service I attended, where a mariachi band supplied the music. The bride was a Lutheran, and the groom was Hispanic—a happy combination of two cultures.

6.

Expectations and Obligations

"ALL YOU HAVE TO DO is show up at the wedding," they might say. Don't believe it. There are protocols, expectations, and just plain nice things for you to do between the time your son tells you he is engaged and the time he takes his wedding vows. There is also that energy you probably feel by being the mother of the groom—the motivation to do things, be involved, and be a vital part of your son's wedding. Now is the time to let that energy express itself.

Becoming Engaged in Your Son's Engagement

Engagement means connecting. By now, you have probably observed the very first protocol expected of the mother of the groom—contacting the bride's family, introducing yourself, and meeting them for dinner or whatever meeting arrangement enables the two families to get together. Try not to limit that contact to just the single obligatory phone call. Follow up where possible with e-mails, pictures, letters, phone calls, and visits. You want to engage and connect with them as you work to lay the foundation for the future.

It's not only your son and his fiancée who are engaged. In a sense, you are also engaged—in planning, in experiencing a new relationship, and in sharing your excitement, questions, and concerns with your family as well as with members of the bride's family.

You will find yourself talking about your son's engagement even if no one has asked. The subject will come up spontaneously with friends, neighbors, and relatives. You'll be ready with an immediate answer when someone asks about your son. It is easy and happy for you to talk about your son's engagement. *Engaged* is something everyone understands and is comfortable with. The relationship has an air of respectability and an almost old-fashioned charm; it speaks of something very sweet, young, and full of promise. The word itself might make you happy. You probably feel a funny kind of pride, almost a sense of satisfaction, when people congratulate you as if you had accomplished something noteworthy. Accept their congratulations, and enjoy the time.

A Time to Celebrate

"It is a wonderful seasoning of all enjoyments to think of those we love."—Molière

Engagement Parties and Showers

This is a time for parties and showers and lunches and dinners, a time to enjoy the company of the people who mean the most to you. You have met her family. Now you will want to introduce your future daughter-in-law to your friends and family, in whatever way geography and time allow.

You can make dinner or have a meal catered at your home, providing an occasion for your close family to meet her. If a birthday or anniversary is coming up, invite your future daughter-in-law and her parents. Social occasions give both families opportunities to see one another, learn each other's names, and know each other better.

Although it's not obligatory, you can also give an engagement party, inviting all your friends and relatives to meet the bridal couple. If the wedding couple lives in Chicago, where the wedding will be held, and you live in Philadelphia, an engagement party may be the only time your friends and family will be able to meet her.

Joyce lived in Boston, and her son was going to be married in the bride's hometown of Cleveland. "I wanted all the people I loved to meet my son and my future daughter-in-law. I knew they couldn't all come to the wedding, so I felt that I wanted to make my own wedding party, and invite everyone." Joyce rented a hall. Instead of having the party catered, she prepared most of the food. Her friends and neighbors helped, bringing food, flowers, wine, and beer. They decorated the hall with photographs of the groom: pictures of him as a toddler, as a twelve-year-old on a bicycle, and as a senior graduating from high school. Joyce asked her future daughter-in-law for pictures of herself growing up so that she could mount them next to her son's. There were also pictures of Joyce and her husband. Joyce's engagement party turned into a wonderful neighborhood celebration, in which she introduced her son's fiancée to almost 100 people and had "the party of my life."

People may or may not bring presents to an engagement party, saving the gift-giving for the wedding. After all, an engagement party, a shower, and a wedding could mean three presents, and that does seem a bit excessive. If anyone asks you, it's courteous and considerate of you to relieve them of the obligation or the possible embarrassment of coming to the party empty-handed. You can find something nice to say, like, "Just come and enjoy yourself." Or, if you're inviting people formally to an engagement party, you can include a message in the invitation, stating, "Please: No presents, just your presence."

A bridal shower is a much smaller event, but it's one that you can also plan, particularly if the bride and her family are far away and many of your friends will not be able to attend the wedding. Her mother's friends, or her own friends where she lives, will probably give her a bridal shower, but you can also give one because this will offer your friends a chance to meet her and to talk with her and to give her the kinds of small and personal presents that every bride likes to have, and that your friends will be happy to give—a casserole dish, a set of monogrammed towels, or a favorite cookbook.

The Rehearsal Dinner

The rehearsal dinner is different. It is your show. Even if you haven't been able to participate in the other activities of the wedding, or if you've been in a quandary about how to participate, this dinner is the one thing that everyone expects you to do.

"The rehearsal dinner is the best part of the wedding," my future daughter-in-law told me. "No performing, no tension, just being with family and friends. Everybody's all psyched up for the big event. People are coming from everywhere, and they're all ready to party."

And it's true. It is your pleasure as well as your responsibility to pick up everyone's excitement and calm everyone's nerves with good food, drink, and camaraderie. A rehearsal dinner brings people together in a joyful new friendship. It brings strangers together so that they might begin to know each other as a family. It brings the members of the wedding party together and helps to relax the powerful emotions let loose by the contemplation of vows and the seriousness of the occasion. As the mother of the groom, you cannot provide a better or more necessary time.

Whom Do You Invite?

"Who *are* these people who are coming from everywhere?" as my daughter-in-law said. Does the rehearsal dinner include the immediate bridal party, who have probably just come from the rehearsal, or does it rightfully include all those people who are coming from everywhere for the ceremony?

You should begin the list with just those people in the wedding party itself—bride and groom; parents, brothers, and sisters with husbands, wives, and significant others; bridesmaids and ushers with husbands, wives, and significant others. You should also include the minister or officiant, and possibly the sexton, the organist, and any other musicians participating in the service—with their husbands, wives, and significant others. At this point, it's still an intimate party. The guests are a small group of people who have a common focus. They are in the wedding, and they need to be together after the rehearsal. This time gives them the chance to get a good feeling for each other's voices and movements and to release their tensions after the rehearsal. It helps ensure that when they meet again the next day at the wedding, they will get it right, and the show will be perfect.

However, if the wedding is held in the bride's territory, far from where you live, and you have invited guests who have traveled a distance, you are responsible for their comfort and amusement. The bride's family may also have guests who have come great distances. What else will they all do on a Saturday night in that little town thirty miles out of Boston, that remote village on Lake Michigan, or in the mountains of upstate New York? You need to invite them to the rehearsal dinner.

As the list grows to include all out-of-towners, the situation gets complicated. You can't be rigid. If the bride's aunt and uncle are out-of-towners but their son lives in the local area, you have to invite him to the party. He and his parents will want to be together. The same goes for the out-of-town daughter and her in-town parents. Flexibility is the operative word.

After you have counted up all the people you want to invite, add a dozen more. Along the way, you will surely decide that someone else should be included—or one of the guests will casually bring along a friend. One of the ushers at mother-of-the-groom Dana's rehearsal dinner called her to ask if he could bring along his brother, who had unexpectedly flown in from Kansas and whom he didn't want to leave alone. It happens, so be prepared.

Where Do You Have This Dinner?

Not all rehearsal dinners have to be held in restaurants. You can make your own dinner at home or have it catered. Janet had the rehearsal dinner in her home, catered by the local delicatessen. She had done the same thing for the couple's engagement party. Her future daughter-in-law had liked it so much, she asked Janet to do it again for her rehearsal dinner. Because everybody in the wedding party was working, Janet decided to give the rehearsal dinner on a Friday night, when they could all relax and put the week behind them. Her dining room table was filled with sandwiches and salads, pickles and potato salad. Everyone in the wedding party was invited; they could even bring friends. This is one way to be a generous host and offer everyone a good time at a picnic supper or at a barbecue in your backyard.

You may also want to give a kind of souvenir gift to everyone at the rehearsal dinner. At a lobster bake on her front lawn, one mother of the groom gave each guest an apron with a big lobster printed on it, along with the names of the bride and groom and the wedding date. Cocktail napkins with wedding bells, the date, and the names of the bride and groom also make for a good souvenir.

If you choose to give the dinner in a restaurant, the hunt should begin months ahead of time. Your choice will depend on several factors: availability, cost, convenience, ambience, and great food. There are lots of questions to ask. Write them down, and keep note of the answers for each location you visit. Here are a few tips:

- You are looking for a restaurant that serves good food at a reasonable cost in a convenient location. Consult a restaurant guide if you don't have a favorite place already in mind. If your future daughter-in-law is more familiar with the location, ask her or her family for recommendations. Italian food is a favorite for many rehearsal dinners. The food is generally good, most people are familiar with the choices, and the costs range from less expensive to more to most. Some people choose Chinese so their guests can read their fortunes.

- If it's at all possible, eat a meal ahead of time at the restaurants on your list. Go with friends so that you can have a good sampling of what is served, the size of the serving, and the quality of the food.

  - Unfortunately, Joan had no choice. Her son was being married in a small town where the bride's family spent

their summers. She lived too far away to visit the restaurant and test their menu. She still winces when she
remembers the wet fish and the dry chicken.

- Cindy and Dave, on the other hand, made a special trip
  to Boston and chose a restaurant in the North End where
  their son and future daughter-in-law used to go for dinner. If you can, it's good to find a place that has some
  special meaning for you or for your son. The familiarity of the place and the memories it evokes add a special
  touch to the occasion. Cindy also liked the neighborhood, with plenty of shops, art galleries, and markets,
  where early guests might like to walk.

- Consider the size of the room and how your guests will be
  seated. Try for an arrangement in which people will have
  the maximum opportunity to talk to each other. Will you
  have a separate room, or will you be assigned several tables
  in a large room with other diners?

  - Clara was planning to invite about forty people to her
    rehearsal dinner. She wanted a Chinese meal so that
    everyone could share and sample different dishes. She vis-
    ited three restaurants before she made her decision. The
    first place, a highly recommended restaurant, was too
    small. They offered her one long table, which could seat
    about twenty-five people, and three smaller tables with
    possibly four at each table. The one long table was "out
    of the question." And just having three small groups of
    four would restrict people's access to each other and not
    allow people to socialize freely. The second restaurant she

visited was a huge Chinese emporium. It was a beautiful and elegantly appointed restaurant, but it seated about 1,200 people, much too large and impersonal for Clara. Fortunately, the third restaurant, also highly recommended, could offer her a private room. That helped her decide.

- Local customs differ from place to place. Nan was surprised when she learned that she was expected to draw up a seating plan for her guests at the rehearsal dinner. In her experience, at rehearsal dinners, guests seated themselves. At the wedding, guests would be assigned tables, but not at the rehearsal dinner. In Atlanta, it was just the opposite: Guests were assigned tables at the rehearsal dinner but not at the wedding reception. Nan did not know about this seating requirement until the day before the dinner. So, if you are a stranger in town, check what is expected early on.

- Is there a view? Choose a view of the sea or gardens, if you can, but also bear in mind that old wisdom that there is an inverse ratio between the quality of the view and the quality of the food. Because most restaurants are enclosed spaces, all you will really want to make sure of is that the space you reserve doesn't have your guests looking into the kitchen or facing the rest rooms.

  - Cindy and Dave chose an Italian restaurant with a private dining room that had a giant mural of the Grand Canal in Venice painted on a long wall across the length of the room so that all the guests looked as if they were sitting beside the gondolas.

- Ambience is an important factor to consider, but beware of those restaurants loaded with atmosphere. The candlelit French restaurant Michelle chose, for instance, was so dark that her guests had a hard time seeing what was on their plates and stumbled to find the rest rooms.
- Check the lighting. Abby had chosen pink roses and lilacs for the tables at her rehearsal dinner. When she entered the room that night, however, she was dismayed to see that the lighting in the room was pink, which drained all the color out of her pink roses.
- Does the restaurant have a parking lot? You will, of course, give driving directions to your guests and trust they will be able to find their way. We now have online mapping websites and GPS instruments to help us. Another way to make sure your guests get back and forth safely is to rent a van or a bus for them. Mary Beth said that was the one thing she would have done differently at her son's wedding. One of her guests, her brother, found himself halfway to New Hampshire before he realized that he had taken the wrong turn. "I should have rented a bus for all my guests. They didn't know their way around, and, after the dinner, after all the drinks, they should not have had to drive along unfamiliar roads back to the hotel."
- As you are looking at the food menu, also look at the wine list. If you intend to serve wine, do you have to supply it or does the restaurant? If the restaurant has a wine list, you can decide now what wines you want them to serve. Do you want an open bar? Talk to the owner or the manager about

wine and liquor questions. If you tell him how many guests are coming, he will probably be able to advise you about the quantity you will need and the cost. Also be sure to find out if you will be charged for bottles that were ordered but not opened.

- Will there be music and flowers? Will there be piped in music, or is there a pianist? Flowers, real ones, are always a plus to any table. Find out if the restaurant provides flowers as part of the table setting or if you have to pay extra for them.

- Don't be shy to talk about costs. Sometimes, the more people you have, the less the cost per person. My husband's favorite question is one he asks doctors as he is about to leave, and one you should ask the maître d', the manager, or the owner: "Is there anything I should know about that I haven't asked you?" You want to have a complete picture of what the evening will look like, sound like, and cost. And then you can decide.

Invitations to the Rehearsal Dinner

You can add a special printed invitation to people who are coming to the rehearsal dinner, maybe even write an informal note, and include it in the same envelope with the wedding invitation. You can wait until you receive the RSVPs and then send a printed invite to the rehearsal dinner. Or, informally, you can phone them or talk to them personally closer to the wedding date when you have a better idea about who is actually coming to the wedding.

The Etiquette Is Engaging

In this interim time before the wedding, you have much to do and think about. You have two primary goals: to introduce your future daughter-in-law and her family to your circle of friends and to your family and to plan a rehearsal dinner. You are engaging everybody who is important to you to participate in one way or another in celebrating your son's wedding. Achieving these goals will bring you much pleasure and satisfaction. It will also allow you entrance into the whirl of the wedding, bringing you closer to the people involved, making you more comfortable with them and better able to participate in the forthcoming event.

7.
Money Matters

MONEY IN THE WEDDING IS the silent, powerful presence that everyone knows is there and that no one really likes to talk about. Who pays for this party? Wedding costs have grown exponentially. Most weddings now are spectacular events that, even on a modest scale, run into thousands of dollars. Who pays for it depends on the finances and the sensitivities of the people involved. Traditionally it was the bride's family, but today the bride and groom frequently assume financial responsibility. But it could also be the groom's family—or a combination of all the parties involved. Your offer to help pay some of the expenses, therefore, will not only be appropriate but more than likely welcome. When you make such an offer, however, you want to be tactful, generous, and gracious. And you can be all three.

The Gift

By tradition, the bride's family pays for the wedding. Even before the cost of weddings escalated, however, it was not uncommon for the groom's parents to offer their son a sum of money and let him and his bride decide how to spend it— either on the wedding itself, on the honeymoon, or on some furnishing for their new home. It was, and still is, in the nature of a wedding present as the parents give their son a handsome check. There's no negotiating here and no need to involve the bride's family.

Looking at Money in a Different Way

"Money, which represents the prose of life, and which is hardly spoken of in parlors without an apology, is in its effects and laws as beautiful as roses."—Emerson

Variations on a Theme

Many different financial scenarios have been used to pay for the wedding, and all are acceptable because you know two things. You would like your son to be married in the kind of wedding that he and his future wife want, and you know that whether it's a simple wedding at home or a ballroom extravaganza, the details add up, and weddings can cost a bundle.

Gina told me that at the very beginning of her son's engagement, the bride's family sat with her and her husband and asked them if they would be willing to share the cost of the wedding, fifty-fifty. It was perfectly all right with Gina, who had expected to contribute and who was pleased and relieved that the money situation was all up front.

On the other hand, Lucille and Frank were a little surprised when, at dinner one night, their son Jon brought up the cost of his forthcoming wedding. He had recently been employed by a banking firm, and his future wife worked as a technical assistant in a television studio. He and she had drawn up an account of the total expenses they anticipated for their wedding. Nothing exorbitant, it was the wedding they wanted and one they thought their parents would enjoy as well. They knew that they could not pay all of the costs without borrowing money. So they decided to ask their parents for financial help. Jon knew his parents well enough to show them the itemized list of expenses and suggested an amount that he thought they might like to contribute.

Although Lucille and Frank were taken a little aback by his business-like approach, they were happy to chip in. Actually, they were even pleased that their son had done his wedding math and had given them a specific amount to contribute. They didn't have to guess, give too little or too much.

Another way to finance the wedding happens on the wedding day itself, when the bride and groom circulate from table to table greeting their guests and making sure that everyone is happy, while, at the same time, receiving checks from all the people who prefer to give money as a present. The groom smiles, puts the envelope in his inside coat pocket, shakes hands with his guest and thanks him very much. It's a time-honored performance and has helped to pay the cost of many a wedding.

Suppose It's Up to You

If nobody says anything to you, what should you do? You can and should initiate this conversation. There's always a certain aura of privacy about money, and with your son or with the bride's family, you want to respect this privacy. When you offer money for something that someone else feels obligated to pay for, you may enter a sensitive territory. People are often self-conscious, embarrassed, or angry when you move into their financial space. Whether you begin the inquiry with your son, your future daughter-in-law, or her parents, soften it with practical suggestions. Don't ask, "Can I help?" Just offer. Try one of these openers or a variation thereof:

- *To your son:* "Jason, Dad and I have been so looking forward to this day. We've put aside a certain amount of money, and we would like you to have it, so that we can all be a part of your dream day. You and Debbie decide how to use it. It would make us very happy."
- *To the bride's family:* "Lorraine, Sam and I have been thinking about the wedding, about how beautiful the plans are, and about how we would like to be part of what you're doing. Tell us what we can take care of—flowers, pictures, wines, limos, music. Where can we fit in?"

Note that these suggestions never imply that the bride's family or the groom need financial help. It's all about the groom's family and their emotional need to be a real part of the wedding. You never imply that the bride's family doesn't have the money; your offer comes out of your wish to participate in the wedding. It's all about sharing the occasion.

Don't be vague or general. Make specific offers, but realize that the decisions are always theirs. Today the wedding costs are often divided like a pie chart, with the bride and groom paying for some things, the bride's family for others, and the groom's family picking up the cost of something else.

Aside from the big wedding tabs, it's also a nice idea to give a small wedding present to your son and to your future daughter-in-law. This might be some item they need to complete their wedding outfit but don't necessarily want to pay for themselves, such as white leather gloves for the bride or a nice pair of black patent leather shoes for the groom.

Avoiding Financial Strain

As the mother of the groom, you are traditionally only expected to provide a rehearsal dinner, something that you can make in your own home where you can control your expenses. You are not obligated to share the cost of the big wedding tabs. Should the bride's family ask you to share the wedding costs, which would be a financial strain for you, you needn't be embarrassed to say that you would rather help in some other important way.

You might offer to do some of the nitty-gritty, time-consuming tasks that would relieve the bride's family. They might like you to do some kind of wedding planner service, such as getting estimates from caterers, printers, florists, and photographers. Or they might appreciate your facilitating travel and hotel arrangements for out-of-town guests, even possibly picking guests up at the airport.

One woman I know baked a variety of cookies, a tradition in her family. Even though the wedding dinner had been catered, she presented plates of cookies at each table during dessert.

The Older Wedding Couple

The times have changed. Many couples are now marrying later in life, in their thirties or forties. They already have established careers, and they can and will pay for their own weddings or good parts of them. Some have been married before and know what they *don't* want this time. They also have their own tastes and know exactly what kind of a wedding they do want. This bride will not turn those decisions over to her mother or to you. Of course, you can always offer to pay for something, but don't be surprised or offended if they say, "Thanks, but we're fine."

When Gladys asked her son if she could help, he said, "No, we can pay for it all." But along the way, he realized he needed money. He didn't hesitate to ask her, and she wasn't at all reluctant to give it to him.

There are some interesting permutations of who pays for the wedding and why. Richard was an executive at IBM, and his fiancée, Frances, was a computer programmer. They were both in their thirties, had never been married before, and could well afford to pay for the huge wedding they wanted. However, both the bride and the groom expected their parents to pay for it. They wanted to follow the tradition of parents' paying for the wedding. They wanted to consider the wedding as their parents' gift. Fortunately, both sets of parents could afford it and went along with the idea.

Check the Bills

Lydia's son Max was marrying Ben's daughter, Gracie, in a destination wedding on the west coast of Mexico. Ben was happy to share the mounting expenses with Lydia and her husband. Both families thoroughly enjoyed the occasion provided by their children. During the reception, Ben, an accountant, sat with Lydia to review all of the expenses and pay the bills. They didn't mind the expensive wines or the specialty cheeses. It was the cost of the bottled water that lifted Ben off his chair. He couldn't believe that so many people had ordered bottles of water. So he and Lydia decided to go around the room and made a visual count of how many bottles of water their guests had actually ordered. They came up with a surprising figure—far less than the number of bottles of water they had been charged for.

The lesson to be learned here is that bills must be checked. In the haze of all these good feelings, don't lose track of what's going on, and don't assume that the numbers you are being presented with are always correct. Add and subtract. Don't be afraid to question the bills.

Money Isn't Always the Issue

Some responses you might get to your offer may have little to do with finances. Beth and her husband were not wealthy, but they were people of means who had built a successful practice. When their son announced his engagement, they spontaneously offered to pay for some of the wedding expenses. The bride's father repeatedly turned them down. This was the same man who had refused to meet with the family because it was "the tax season." He insisted that he would pay for the wedding, that he had a budget for the wedding, and that the wedding costs be held within his budget.

Beth repeatedly tried to contribute something. It was not just about money. It was a deeply personal matter. It was about wanting to involve herself and her husband in her son's wedding. As the wedding plans were being finalized, she decided to try once more. "We would so much like to contribute something. Isn't there anything we can give—flowers, musicians, photographers, limos?" "Yes," answered the bride's father with a slight smile, "you can pay for all your guests." And he actually meant it! Who knows what motivated that answer? Money is a source of power; it gives one a sense of security, self-importance, and status.

Money Oils the Machinery

It is important for you to be aware of the expenses of your son's wedding and not to rely on the traditional notion that wedding costs are essentially the bride's dowry. With tact and understanding, you should offer to contribute some financial help or pick up the cost of some part of the wedding. In most cases, the bride's family, as well as the bride and groom, will welcome it.

Even if you know the bride's family can afford this wedding, your offer will be appreciated. It demonstrates that you really want to be a part of this family and this event. It will also make it easier for you to be included in many of the discussions and decisions that will take place later on about the wedding. As Byron wrote, "Ready money is Aladdin's lamp."

8.

Invitations and Whom to Invite

THE INVITATION IS NOT JUST a piece of paper. The wedding invitation heralds the event. It involves countless micro-decisions, each one revealing who you are and how you would like to be presented. Although the bride's family is usually responsible for the wedding invitations, you will be more than an interested party. It is a courtesy for the mother of the bride to discuss the look of the invitation and the wording with you. However, if she doesn't, it's not out of order for you to talk with her about it.

The wording of the invitation, its design, and the recipients will soon become an integral part of your daily conversations.

Design Decisions

Traditionally, wedding invitations were printed in black script on ivory bond, hidden in layers of tissue and double envelopes. That's how they used to come to me. Not so any more.

Before you become involved with the wording of the invitation, consider the many options for the color, design, and size of the invitation. You might take the time to visit a printer, look at catalogs, and see what choices are available. Do a little homework before you talk to the bride's family or to the couple so that you know something about possibilities and costs. Remember that one plan is not better than another. How you and the couple want the invitation to read and to look are matters of personal choice relating to the way all of you want to appear on paper.

The invitation to my cousin's wedding was a photograph of two birds flying over the beach with a love poem by Christina Rossetti in the lower right-hand corner. How perfect! Howard, a child of the seventies, lives in Southern California and practices homeopathic medicine. His wedding invitation perfectly represented him.

Jessie and Bert chose a traditional black script, with the requisite tissue paper and double envelopes. Father is a lawyer. Mother is a Realtor. They live in a Westchester suburb and are very conscious of status and appearances. They are most happy with traditions.

Hazel's future daughter-in-law, Miranda, an artist, used an abstract floral design as the cover of her wedding invitation.

It was a reproduction of a painting Miranda had once given to her mother for a birthday present. Her decision to use that painting pleased Hazel not only because it was beautiful but also because it was a personal statement—almost like a gift to everyone who would receive it.

You Are Cordially Invited

Mothers and fathers remarry, and names change. The wording of an invitation reveals an intricate puzzle of family relationships and personal statements. This is especially true today, when many parents are no longer married to the same people with whom they had their children. What names and how many will be used in your son's invitation?

Usually, the text begins with an invitation from the bride's family. But you, too, can share top billing. For many parents of the groom, it is important for the wording of the invitation to indicate that the groom's family also wants to invite people to their son's wedding.

How you identify yourself if you have been previously married also needs clarification. Vicki had remarried after a divorce from Brad's father. Like many other women in her situation, she wanted people to know that she was Brad's mother even though their last names were now different. She also didn't like the formality of the "Mrs." followed by her husband's name, which would then totally obscure her own identity. Ultimately, she decided to use her first name followed by her first married name and then her current married name. That made her comfortable and gave everyone all the necessary information.

The wording could then include the names of the bride's family and the names of the groom's family and would read like this: "Jacqueline and Thomas Davis and Vicki Simmons Benning and Alfred Benning request the pleasure of your presence at the wedding of our children, Sandra Davis and Brad Simmons."

Or, if you prefer something more formal, "Mr. and Mrs. James Fogarty and Mr. and Mrs. Geoffrey Gardner request the honor of your presence at the marriage of their daughter, Sherri Ann Fogarty, to Samuel Paul Gardner."

If the groom's mother is widowed, her name appears alone in the joint invitation.

Now you are no longer invisible or, as one mother of the groom described herself, "a third-class citizen." If your name is included as one of the inviters to the wedding, the wording of the invitation not only informs people of who you are, it also reveals something positive about the relationship between the two families.

Invitation Disagreements

Most often, families can agree on what should be said and how. Occasionally, however, the wording of the text can produce or reveal a strain in the relationship.

Natalie, the mother of the groom, had many arguments and differences with the bride's family. When the wedding invitations were being planned and the mother of the bride, in a conciliatory offer, suggested a joint family wording, Natalie refused it. Because the bride's family had been unwilling to let her participate in any of the planning, Natalie was angry and simply said, "It's your wedding, not ours."

This was not a good attitude. She should have tried to look ahead. While we can appreciate her frustration, here was an opportunity that might have changed the whole climate of the wedding preparations for the groom's family. It might also have helped mend the future of their relationship to the bride's family. For whatever reason, perhaps a sense of guilt or an attempt to mend fences, the mother of the bride was opening a door. The mother of the groom should not have slammed it shut.

For Polly and Robert, the reverse situation was true. They were both successful dentists. Their son was just starting out in his own practice and was marrying the only child of a single mother, an interior decorator with a lifestyle of her own and very definite ideas about how she wanted the wedding to look. She would take care of all the details of the wedding, beginning with the invitation.

But because Polly and Robert were paying for most of the wedding, and since this was their only son, Polly felt that they should be included in the opening lines of the invitation, not just relegated to the bottom of the page as the groom's parents. The bride's mother, however, refused to change the wording, even over the pleadings and the anger of her future son-in-law and regardless of the financial contribution being made by his family. It was her daughter's wedding, and she insisted that the invitation come only from her.

In a situation like this, what can you do? For one thing, Polly might have made a personal appeal to the bride's mother, talking directly with her rather than using her son as the mediator. She also might have come up with some suggested compromise wording. The point is that she should have gone one step beyond her son's attempt, but she didn't because she was too afraid of any conflict. So the wedding invitation went out as the bride's mother wanted it to, leaving Polly with stinging memories for years to come.

Whom Do You Invite?

It's a time to ponder relationships. Relatives are probably first on the list. If you're lucky, you may have a few close ones. The rest sort of fan out in a widening arc, further and further away from you. Friends are important. Close, closer, closest. Neighbors? Coworkers? Ideally, you want to invite a circle of people for whom this event will be important. It will be important to them because both you and your son are important to them. Years from now you want to remember this time with them, to look at pictures with them and to retell the stories.

On the wall in Pat and Sean's dining room is a framed light-blue poster listing the names of all the people who came to their wedding. "We loved them, and we just wanted them to be with us always."

The More the Merrier?

"Wine maketh merry; but money answereth all things."
—Ecclesiastes 10:19

Expanding and Contracting

If the bride's family or the bride and groom are paying most of the bills, you need to ask how many guests you might invite—unless, of course, you have already been told. You want to respect the numbers unless you also offer to pay for more guests. But if you want to keep the numbers within reason, you will find yourself assessing the gradations of friendship, going from the ones you want to invite to the ones you must invite (including all those you know will not come), giving way gradually to the ones you should invite (but probably won't), slowly descending to those who, you're sure, would be insulted if they weren't invited. Would they really be insulted? Would you then feel guilty meeting them in the supermarket or getting a Christmas card from them? Lots of questions will go round and round in your mind.

Making up lists of people to invite can easily become a favorite pastime. You examine all your relationships, blood and otherwise. As you begin to think of your greater family, be prepared to find yourself hesitating a little at the thought of introducing some of them to this new family on the horizon. You see a cousin who eats too much, a sister who is boring, an uncle who has too many opinions, an aunt who has none. It's best to accept them all and know that, as beautiful and bright as she is, your future daughter-in-law must have some two-headed people in her family.

The fun of a party depends on the people who are there. So you then look to your wide world of friends: long-time friends, new friends, friends who knew your son when he was a little boy even if they haven't seen him in twenty-five years. If you have limits, consider the connections between your friends and your son. After all, you want him to enjoy their presence at his wedding. Here's a sample list of criteria to help you decide:

- You don't want to invite people your son has never seen. He can invite people you don't know, but try not to invite too many people *he* doesn't know.
- Have they ever had dinner at your house with him?
- Can he talk easily to them?
- Does he like them? Although you might feel comfortable inviting them to your house for dinner, would your son want them at his wedding?
- Share your list with him. Although you don't need to have him approve your guest list, he should know who is on it and be pleased with it. He might even ask you to include someone you had forgotten but who might be important to him and whom he might want to be there.

Some Issues Need Airing

The question of whom her son would or would not want at his wedding became a critical and painful issue for Rebecca, whose son refused to let her make up her own guest list. He told her whom to invite and whom not to. She was appalled but did nothing about it. I asked her why she and her son didn't talk this one out. She said she didn't want to argue with him and create a problem; after all, it was his wedding.

I thought otherwise. She should have talked very honestly to him about the issues in this wedding list, the importance of being fair to her. The differences between her list and his could have been negotiated if she had been honest with him and secure with her own feelings and decisions.

In all of these preparations for your son's wedding, you can anticipate that there will be some differences between what you would like and what he, his bride, or his bride's family would like. Don't be afraid of these differences. Most can be discussed and negotiated. Some you must be willing to accept. But some battles are worth having. They clear the air and let everybody know what's going on. It's also not bad to disagree with your son along the way. He needs to know what you feel most strongly about. He also needs to realize that although he and his bride are the central figures in the event, the wedding is not just about them. It's also about families and community.

An honest argument will never jeopardize your relationship with your son. But a long persistent grievance will.

Solving Some Guest-List Puzzles

The guest list grows exponentially when you find that there are layers of guests all connected to each other. You find yourself starting sentences like, "Well, if you invite Bernie, then you must ask . . ." It's not unheard of to make up two guest lists, an "A" list and a "B" list. When you get regrets from someone on the "A" list, you plug in the "B" list, hoping that the parties never meet and casually discuss when they got their invitations. You can also invite some people only to the service, which might include wine and cake afterward, but not to the full reception and the dinner. Or you might choose to do the opposite, especially if the wedding service is private, and only invite people to the reception. Here are two examples of invitations for these two circumstances:

For the ceremony only
"Mr. and Mrs. George Davis Langhorne and Mr. and Mrs. Jerome Ashwood request the honor of your presence at the wedding service of their children, Jenna to Christopher Francis Ashwood."

For the reception only
"George and Ellen Langhorne and Jerry and Susan Ashwood are pleased to invite you to join them at a reception in honor of their daughter Jenna's marriage to Christopher Francis Ashwood."

You can go formal or informal in your wording and can choose to spell "honour" British style, with the "u," or not.

A question always comes up regarding the people who have invited you to their children's weddings. Are you obligated to return the invitation? Not necessarily. Yes, you have given their children expensive presents, but don't think of this as payback time. Whether or not you invite them to your son's wedding should depend on how emotionally close to them you really are.

Martha recalls an argument with her son, who didn't understand why she wanted to invite all of her friends to a wedding that he wanted to keep very private and strictly for the immediate family.

"He thought I wanted to invite my close friends because I had given all their children wedding presents and now I wanted them to give my son presents. But it really wasn't about 'payback time.' We gave each other's children bridal showers with everything they needed for the kitchen, the bathroom, and the bedroom, and then for the wedding—always a big check. We were friends, and we did that for each other out of friendship. It was an unwritten code among us, to help the children. Inviting them to my son's wedding would give them the long-anticipated opportunity to show their love and friendship for me. It was important for me to invite them."

Martha was not afraid to explain her feelings to her son. She wasn't afraid of a conflict or an argument but spoke honestly and deeply to him. Her son listened and understood. Ultimately, both were very happy to have her friends at the wedding. And her friends were happy to be there.

If the wedding will be held far from where you and most of your friends live, you have to consider the cost to your friends in terms of hotels, motels, planes, and trains—not to mention a day or two away from work.

Louise wanted to invite Catherine to her son's wedding. Catherine always lived on the edge of poverty and was afraid of losing her current job. Two nights in a hotel, food, a present, and so on might be a financial imposition. But not receiving an invitation at all might make her feel even worse than having to turn it down. Louise finally decided to invite Catherine and let her decide. When Catherine accepted the invitation, Louise introduced her to Molly, another local friend who was driving to the wedding. At least she saved Catherine the plane fare.

Although it is not expected or necessary, some parents of the groom assume the expense of hotel bills for the guests who have to come a distance and cannot stay with one or another relative in the area. Whether you are paying for their expenses or not, it is your responsibility to help locate reasonable quarters for your out-of-town guests.

Other questions about whom to invite will require your decisions and your assistance. What about your friends with health problems? How will they get to the wedding? Will some people drive? Can they car pool? Are you going to invite the nieces with babies who probably can't come? Ditto for the cousins who might not be able to get away from work.

What do you do about inviting friends who are in the midst of a divorce or who have just been divorced? Should you invite one, the other, or both? In one situation, the mother of the groom decided that although she liked both of them, since she had known the husband longer than his ex-wife, she would only invite him. She also mistakenly believed that the ex-wife would be uncomfortable at a wedding where her ex-husband would also be a guest. Instead of making everybody comfortable, as she imagined she would, she deeply hurt the ex-wife who resented not being invited and who, several months later, told her that it wouldn't have bothered her at all to see her ex at the wedding.

Nina and Ben had friends who had been lovers for fifteen years until the man broke up the relationship by marrying someone else. Nina and Ben were still very friendly with his former girlfriend as well as with him and his new wife. Nina decided to invite them all—the former lover and the new couple. She also let them know that she was inviting all of them. "Each of them appreciated being invited. They were so happy that I hadn't excluded any of them out of a false sense of embarrassing anyone. They could handle it better than I could."

When it comes to broken relationships, you can't judge how people will feel. You could begin by asking whether people mind your inviting the ex. Or you could just tell all parties involved what you would like to do and let them decide how comfortable they would be accepting the invitation.

ABOUT INVITATIONS

- The invitation is a formal announcement, an area where you can and should have some input. Your contribution to how it looks and what it says can be a good opportunity to be part of the planning for your son's wedding. Don't be afraid to share ideas and ask questions. Trust your own responses and talk about them with your husband, your son, your future daughter-in-law, and her family.

- Wedding invitations can be worded in many ways. Before you begin this discussion with the bride's family, write up several options that make you comfortable. You might even visit a printer or a stationery store to get some ideas.

- Enjoy making a list of the people you want to invite to the wedding, but respect the number limit and allow the bride and groom to have the longer guest list.

- Don't get caught in the trap of feeling that you should be able to invite just as many people to the wedding as the bride's family invites. If the wedding is in the bride's neighborhood, which might be far from yours, it's only logical that her family will invite many more people to the wedding than you will.

- You can't second-guess how people will respond to an invitation. Always respecting the numbers, invite those people you want to be there as well as those who want to be there. Let invitees decide for themselves whether they *can* be there.

Ultimately, you want to be happy with the people you invite. Your guests should be the people you would like to introduce to your future daughter-in-law and people with whom you would really like to party on your son's wedding day.

9.
Be Involved Without Interfering

IT CAN BE HARD TO know how to help graciously without taking the reins away from the bride and her family. You don't want to act like a backstage manager. Rather, you're waiting in the wings to take care of this and that, someone whose opinions and help are sought or offered but never pushed or imposed.

Of course, there are the professionals—the printers, caterers, florists, wedding planners—who are there to help the families decide, and, too often, to make the decisions for them. Their suggestions, however, are just that. In the flurry and pressure of spending so much money, don't feel intimidated by the pros or by your fear of making a horrible and expensive mistake.

Creating Many Opportunities to Talk

The first, easiest, and most important thing for you to do in the planning of the wedding is to keep in touch with all the players. Trust your own responses and talk about them with your husband, son, future daughter-in-law, and her family. You demonstrate your interest and your wish to be involved by keeping close to what is happening.

But also remember not to step over the line. You can follow the details without intruding or trying to control. Don't be invisible. Simple phone calls and e-mails make it possible for you to ask questions and to offer reasonable responses at just the right moments. Although you can anticipate problems, you can't always anticipate the complications that may arise as the situation evolves. There will most often be aspects of the problem you couldn't have imagined earlier. There is always the unexpected.

Remember, if it's possible, to keep those dinner and lunch dates going with the bride's family, whether at a restaurant, at your house, or theirs. These meetings don't have to coincide with a holiday or a birthday. In fact, the less formal, the better. If the couple lives a distance from you, find a weekend when they can visit just for fun.

The talk will almost certainly be about the wedding, but it doesn't have to be. Sometimes wedding issues are solved through specific discussions, but solutions also come at unexpected moments. Creative people describe how they can walk away from a problem and become involved in something totally unrelated, when suddenly the answer appears. Provide many casual occasions to get together just to talk, about anything and everything. In that talk, you might discover mutually satisfying solutions.

Talk About Flowers

Deciding on flowers and selecting flowers provide a natural opening for you to become involved.

Corsage, Wristlet, or Bouquet?

Either the bride's mother or the bride will probably initiate this conversation. You may want your hands free of a bouquet—one hand possibly to hold your son's and the other to hold a handkerchief. There's no such thing as a trivial detail in the planning of a wedding.

A corsage? "No!" said Georgina. "I'm too short-waisted, and I have a full bosom." The mother of the bride didn't want to wear a corsage either because her dress was a flowered print. Flowers are always lovely. But too many flowers—the corsage and the floral pattern of her dress—would be over the top, literally. Another factor Georgina considered was the fabric of her dress. It was chiffon, sheer and light, and the corsage would weigh it down.

By giving an honest response, the mother of the groom encouraged the mother of the bride to give her true feelings. Resolving such a small detail had them laughing and brought them closer together.

Wristlets were a very serious consideration for Julia. She didn't want to wear one, but it was very important to her future daughter-in-law, who insisted on them for both mothers to distinguish them from the other wedding guests. Everyone would see that they were being honored in a special way.

Although Julia had a bracelet she wanted to wear on one wrist and an elegant watch on the other, eventually she wore a wristlet to please the bride. Under the pressure to make everything perfect, each detail takes on exaggerated importance.

The Generosity of Spirit

"You give but little when you give of your possessions. It is when you give of yourself that you truly give."—Kahlil Gibran

Flowers in the Ceremony

Selecting the flowers is a huge and personal responsibility. This task often goes to the bride's mother. So many decisions are piled on top of her that she might be relieved to have help deciding what flowers to choose and how many would go where. But you have to offer gently.

It doesn't take long to realize that the cost of flowers adds up quickly. Just looking at the altar and chapel is intimidating as you consider the spaces that need to be filled and you count the number of pews. Here is an opportunity for you to offer financial as well as practical advice. You don't have to decorate all of the pews—perhaps only the first ten or twelve rows, depending on how many guests you think will fill them. The altar should have flowers but can also have plants and grasses as well as ferns.

Having a *huppa* raises the question of more flowers. Some people cover it totally with flowers. This is beautiful, but it's also expensive and not really cost effective because, from the congregation's viewpoint, the flowers are hardly visible. Instead of flowers, however, you can use a decorative cloth that has special meaning for you or a prayer shawl—a *tallis*. If you are looking for meaningful ritual, your suggestion to use a *tallis* instead of flowers is perfect.

But each wedding drama is a different play, and not everyone is always welcomed into the script so graciously. Maggie is wonderful with flowers. She has a beautiful garden and loves working with green things. She's creative, and she knows a great deal about flowers, plants, and trees. When her son Evan was married, she joyfully volunteered to take care of the flowers—to select, pay for, and arrange them. It was her gift to her only son.

The bride's mother, however, refused to allow her to do this. She had a color scheme in mind with very specific flowers and how she wanted to arrange them. Maggie threw up her hands. "They were in charge," she told me. "It's not my show. I've been brought up well and know what manners are. I don't want to make waves. Just be a lady and be supportive. That's my role." She smiled wryly at me. "But I did get to decorate the tables at the rehearsal dinner." If you can't win one battle, maybe you can win another.

Flowers on the Tables

The tables at the reception present another costly flower scene. However, there are many inexpensive and attractive ways to prepare a table setting. This is the time for you to buy magazines and read decorating books. Study the world of table settings, and you will become conversant with many beautiful possibilities.

Instead of flowers at each table, mother-of-the-groom Janice suggested ivy topiaries as centerpieces with votive candles, black olives, and breadsticks on either side. She had gotten the idea from a magazine and decided to execute it for her son's wedding reception. It can be fun to think about flowers and to look at all the stunning photographs; just be sure to keep the bride and groom's tastes in mind.

Feel free to ask the bride or her mother what they're planning to do and enter the conversation. But have some ideas ahead of time to literally bring to the table, and then you can offer to help. If you have a garden, you can offer fresh-cut flowers to place on the tables or to use as decorations in tall vases in corners of the room. It's your very own contribution. When her son's wedding took place in early spring, Carol, a science teacher, cut dozens of daffodils and put them in small flasks she borrowed from the high school's science lab. She placed the flasks like ribbons down the center of each table.

A Candid Opportunity

Most likely the bride's family will have made arrangements for the official photos of the wedding—studio portraits, still shots of the bridal party, or a video of the ceremony. But you can offer to present a different picture memory of the wedding by giving the couple a wedding album of candid shots you and your friends have taken. Prior to the wedding date, you can ask several of your friends who will have their cameras there to share their wedding shots with you. Then you can select the ones you like best, buy a beautiful album, and present it to the returning honeymooners.

Do You Have Any Connections?

Whom do you know? Do you have any personal contacts with a florist, printer, limo driver, or wine distributor? If you haven't already thought of it, this is the time to share your connections with the bride's family.

Who Sits Where?

The seating arrangement at the reception is another fascinating problem to solve. Of course, in some wedding receptions, the guests find their own places. That's easy. But in most receptions, the guests are assigned to tables. You can offer to help with the seating arrangement.

"It's a lot of work, and everyone gets mad at you," said Harisse, who was asked by the bride's family if she would be willing to do this. "But it's a wonderful way to get to know the guests, and it's a big help to the bride and her family."

The first step is to meet with the bride and her family so that you can learn their wishes. You can then get together to explore the many possibilities of seating arrangements. Should the bride's and the groom's guests each sit at their own assigned tables? It makes a kind of sense: People know each other, and talk is easy and familiar. But what about mix and match? Then people can have new conversations, different from the ones they have been having with each other every Saturday night. And then, too, the families would have a chance to meet and remember each other long after the wedding.

No matter what plan you choose, the problems and questions attendant to seating people call upon every social strategy you have. Should young marrieds sit together, given that they have so much in common? How about the singles? (When I was single, being invited to a friend's wedding was a great opportunity to meet eligible men.)

Couples usually are assigned to the same table, but not former lovers. Old aunts and uncles should be mixed in with everybody else to prevent the formation of an old folk's table. What about lawyers at the same table, and all the doctors at another? They would all have something to say to each other. Then again, people might not like to get caught up in shop talk and the insidious competitive small talk that sometimes creeps into such conversations.

Then there is the matter of personality. Working together on the seating plan, you will soon learn who is boring, who is fun to be with, who is uncomfortable with strangers, who is always competing for attention. Should you sprinkle the tables evenly with interesting talkers, bright spots? Should you scatter the dull ones or gather them together and let them bore each other? Should you seat Uncle Joe next to Aunt Betsy? They haven't spoken to each other in years. Is this a good time for them to get over it? Maybe not.

Figuring out the puzzle gives you a great opportunity to talk to the bride and her mother. Of course, while you are discovering all the quirks in their family, they will learn the truth about yours. By the time you will have shuffled the deck several times, neither family will have any more illusions about the other. It's a serious challenge, but it's also fun along the way. The real accomplishment of the task is bigger than just making a seating plan. It provides you with an honest opportunity to bond with the bride's family.

Even if you are not asked to help with the seating plan, it is wise for you to understand where you and your guests will be seated. Will you be on a dais or at Table #1? Will your guests be seated at tables throughout the room or in one area? You might want to request that they not be seated too close to the band or tucked away in corners. Or maybe at this reception, tables are not assigned, and guests seat themselves. It's good to know ahead of time so that you are prepared for the scene and able to help if needed.

Preparing the Place Cards

A small but essential service that would relieve the bride's family from another task and expense has to do with preparing the place cards. The bride's family most often chooses the kind of place cards they like and the number they anticipate needing. You can help by offering to check prices and by bringing a selection of ideas to choose from. A good printer will have a book of possible styles and colors and may even give you some good advice.

You can, of course, pick a graphic design, buy the blank cards, and let your computer do the work. Isabelle, who had a talent for drawing, offered to design the place cards for her son's wedding. She was not only an artist but a skilled calligrapher. Even if you don't have Isabelle's artistic talent, if you have good handwriting, you might offer to do the job.

Perhaps the best time to offer this suggestion is when the deadline for RSVPs has been met. Always remember to order more than you think you need—just in case.

Unexpected Service

You may find yourself unexpectedly playing a different role— the role of the mother of the bride.

The bride's mother usually goes with her daughter to buy her gown, plan the reception, work out the guest list, and share with her all the thousand decisions that make the wedding day happy and beautiful. But what if the mother of the bride isn't there or doesn't want to be there?

Cathy's son Edward was marrying Elizabeth, whose mother was remarried and living in Oklahoma. Elizabeth was the third daughter of her mother's first marriage. Her mother was simply not interested in her; she was living her own life in a place very far away from Elizabeth. So it was up to Cathy to fill that space and be the mother that Elizabeth needed in this critical time of her life.

Beth filled the same role for her future daughter-in-law, Judy, for different reasons. Judy and her parents had so many conflicts about the wedding—where it should be, who should come, how much to spend—that Judy could no longer talk easily to her mother about the wedding. She needed a shoulder to cry on. Beth sympathized with her and provided that shoulder.

This was not an easy situation for Beth. On the one hand, she did not want Judy to be estranged from her own parents; nor did she want Judy's parents to blame her for the problems between them and their daughter. She also did not want there to be hard feelings between the two families. But Beth genuinely loved the young woman who was marrying her son, a young woman who was alone and literally crying for help. Beth was able to act as a comfort zone for Judy; a woman Judy could talk to. She also helped to give Judy the confidence and support she needed to plan her own wedding. But, equally important, Beth helped her to overcome her frustrations and anger and find a positive way to deal with her parents.

A Wedding Watcher

If you happen to attend any weddings during the months before your son is married, you will find yourself becoming acutely conscious of all the details surrounding the wedding and the reception. You will be sensitive to what is working nicely as well as to the possibilities for disaster. One wedding watcher told me she made mental notes of some problems she saw at a reception and shared them with her son and with the bride's family. "The devil lives in the details," she said as she found herself asking questions like these:

- If there are candles on the altar, has someone been designated to light them?
- If hors d'oeuvres are being served buffet style, how can you avoid having people crowd into a small area?
- How far should the musicians be from the reception area so that people will be able to talk to each other when the music is playing?
- If there is going to be a champagne toast, has someone been assigned to filling the glasses so that they are ready for the toast?

You Are Not Always Needed

There will, however, be many occasions when you are not involved and when your advice is not being sought. One of the invaluable lessons you learn during this planning-for-the-wedding time is that your son and future daughter-in-law are adults with good judgment, quite capable of making important decisions. He can choose wines and select the menu. They do know to put up a special table for the children. They have arranged for the champagne and the limo. Yes, they know it will cost more, but they prefer a band to a DJ. They have a photographer, and no, he will not hunchback his way down the aisle, setting the pace of the procession.

They have already answered most of your questions. You may learn to sense the irritation in your future daughter-in-law's voice as you hear yourself asking for the third time whether the band will play during or after the soup. Just remember that this is their day, and they know what they're getting themselves into.

A Time to Build

So much to do, to think about. And how quickly the time goes. But it is an important time. It's your time to become involved in this important event of both your son's life and your life. During these weeks and months, when you and he talk, you will begin to see a new relationship developing between you. You are solving problems together. He will listen to you differently, not as his mother. You will talk to him differently, not exactly like mother to son. It is the information you are sharing, the problems you are solving, that are important. Your relationship to each other is evolving, and there's a new friendship between you, something very nice and adult. It's your reward.

10.

The Wedding Look

WEDDINGS PROVIDE ONE OF THE few occasions most of us have in our casual lifestyle to dress up in fantasy clothes, with flowers, satin and lace, and long white gloves. Even the men buy patent-leather shoes and trade in their navy-blue blazers and khaki slacks for black-and-white tuxedos, dinner jackets, or morning coats. What you choose to wear suddenly becomes one of the most crucial decisions in your life. There's the image and then there's you. How to merge the two and be a beautiful part of the wedding pageant—that's the challenge.

How Much Time Do You Have?

"We're getting married in May, Mother." That's why my son told me in December, which gave me about five months to process the information and buy a dress. The amount of time you have in which to buy "the dress" varies. I had five months. You

145

may have more than a year, given that many couples have to pick a date far in advance in order to get the hall or the church they want. Or your son may tell you on Friday afternoon that he's getting married on Sunday. How much time you have will certainly affect your shopping choices.

What Do Mothers Wear?

"A skirt should be tight enough to show you're a woman, but loose enough to show you're a lady."—Michele Slung

The only words of advice I had ever heard addressed to the mother of the groom were these: "Just wear beige and don't say anything." Silence aside, suppose you don't want to wear beige or you look awful in beige. You begin to click off your memory of weddings you have attended and try to remember the look of mothers coming down the aisle. Some were sweet looking, in flowing soft fabrics; others had a tailored look, a suit or a long skirt with a silk brocade jacket.

Recent articles on wedding fashions report a changing attitude with a variety of options for mothers of the groom to choose from. One fashion article reports that although many mothers still prefer neutral colors like beige, dusty pink, and pale blue, others are requesting black. Another fashion account extols a sophisticated and sexy look revealing bare backs, cleavage, and curves, a youthful and glamorous look featuring hand-beaded gowns, décolleté corset tops, strapless dresses with slits up the back or the side. Some bridal shop owners see a trend toward hot and iridescent colors like copper, cranberry, wine and burgundy, or bronze and antique gold—a shiny look. All agree that mothers want luxurious fabrics like silk, tissue-taffeta, organza, and lace. Only occasionally do mothers these days choose a classic dress with a jacket.

Coordinating Your Outfit with the Bridal Party

To begin the hunt, you must first find out if the wedding is organized around a color scheme. The bride's decisions set the tone and maybe even the colors of the wedding party. In some weddings, the bride wants everybody to wear black and white, or pink and green. Her decision will at least give you some direction. Even if you are free to choose whatever color you want, you still need to begin your search by discussing colors with the bride and with her mother.

Loretta's future daughter-in-law had selected her wedding dress—a white off-the-shoulder *peau de soie* with a tight-fitting bodice, a full skirt, and a bustle in the back. She wanted her three bridesmaids to wear pastel colors made of the same material, also with a bustle in the back. She had set the tone of the wedding. It was to be formal, and the women would wear gowns. If you wore a suit in that wedding procession, you would want it to be an evening suit, something elegant with a long skirt.

You're not in competition with the bride's mother, but knowing what she is wearing may influence what you choose. Your choice might also help her to decide on a dress. It's good to have an ongoing conversation with her during this grand shopping time. When you know what color her dress is or whether it's patterned in flowers or has stripes, you can better decide what you want to look for. She's likely very curious about your dress. Talking to each other about clothes and colors is also fun—and yet another way to bring your two families together. Both of you want the same thing. You each want to look beautiful and be part of a beautiful ensemble piece.

If there is no unifying color scheme, no special requests from the bride, and no need to coordinate with the bride's mother, then you're off and running into wide-open territory. There are so many choices that you may wish they had told you to wear blue.

Creating the Image

What do you want to look like coming down the aisle? Your best, of course! But what exactly is that? You may have a cocktail party "best," a "best" for dinners out, and yet another "best" for concerts or the opera. What would be the "best" for your son's wedding?

Because you may be first in the order of the processional march, you have a special advantage, maybe even a responsibility, to set the tone of the procession. It's your job to make way for the star, who we all agree is the bride.

Laura told me of her journey to find the perfect dress. She felt that it was inappropriate for the mother of the groom to be flamboyant. She didn't want to make everybody look at her or to get the same attention as the bride. "I didn't want to make a fashion statement. I really wanted to look like a quiet, digni- fied, and elegant lady. Maybe the idea of becoming a mother-in- law had matured me? Or was I remembering some old movie with Deborah Kerr?"

For many women, the search for the perfect dress can be arduous, disillusioning, and frightfully expensive. "I felt I had to buy an expensive dress," Sandy told me. " My friends and all the people I worked with urged me to go for the best. You know, a once-in-a-lifetime dress. So I spent a huge amount of money for it—navy blue moiré with lace over the bodice. Floor length, of course. My husband said I looked beautiful in it. So I bought it. I've never worn it again. I don't have the kind of social life in which I could wear a dress like that. Besides, because I've gained a little weight, I'll never be able to fit into it again. The dress is wrapped in cellophane and hangs in the back of my closet. Was it worth it? I don't know."

Kerry and Mike, a Japanese-American couple who live in California, had a different experience. Their son Matt was mar- rying Annie, whose parents lived in South Korea. At the insis- tence of Annie's family, Kerry and Mike were forced to buy expensive wedding clothes. They were even told how much they should each spend—at least $3,000 for the mother's gown and almost as much for the father's suit. For the American couple, typical casual Californians, these demands were an outrage. For the Korean parents, however, these requests were critical in considering an appropriate suitor for their daughter.

Expensive clothes were a demonstration of wealth. The family needed to be assured that their daughter was marrying into a respectable family, worthy of her and of her family.

The Search Is On

"Go ahead and try it on. You can't compare yourself to a hanger."—Michele Slung

Time to Shop

Some women have their dresses made to order. Most of us go shopping. It's wise to take along a friend, someone who will tell you truthfully how you look and someone you can enjoy lunch with afterward. You can even ask your daughter-in-law to go shopping with you. That could provide a very nice and intimate opportunity to build a real friendship.

First you will probably try the specialty bridal shops. Laura went to one and found an apricot chiffon possibility, but in the wrong size. The saleswoman said, "Don't worry, we can alter to fit." Beware—there's always a dressmaker on the premises who can shorten it, lengthen it, open it up, or take it in. But is it wise to buy an expensive dress and then have it completely remade? Will it ever look as it was intended, or will you be forever fussing with that pleat in the front that just doesn't fall right?

After the specialty shops come the department stores. On a January after-the-holiday sale rack, Laura found a jade-green chiffon two-piece tea-length dress that had been twice reduced. "It had a slip-like taffeta top and double-tiered skirt with an over-blouse that fell to the hips, creating a drop waist look. Very slenderizing. It had short sleeves and a bateau neckline. The fabric was patterned with little squares edged in gold thread. I liked it immediately, but I thought it might not be appropriate for a wedding. It was more like a party dress, not at all what I had had in mind. It wasn't reserved, quiet, or dignified. Besides, it was too cheap, twice reduced!" Laura asked if she could take the dress home on approval and so that she could look at herself without the pressure of the department store mirror. At home, she still liked the dress, but she continued to shop for another month until she exhausted both herself and all the stores in the area. She finally accepted her good luck in finding the right dress at the right price. "I bought it."

Get rid of the idea that you have to spend a lot of money for a dress. In fact, considering all the other expenses you have incurred as part of the wedding, getting a bargain should make you feel terrific. There are two kinds of shoppers. There's one who recognizes a good purchase and buys it right away, and then there's the one who thinks there's always something better in the next store. Try to be the first kind.

You will always find lots of beige (wheat, natural, cream), mauve, and periwinkle, especially when you tell the salesperson that you are the mother of the groom. You can look for months. The "better dresses," or what are commonly called "occasion dresses," section is a world of sequins, beads, and lace. One mother of the groom described the dress she had been shown. "It was a long green gown with layers of flounces from the knees down," she said. "The salesperson told me I would be 'stunning' coming down the aisle. I took the dress home and when my son saw it, he practically laughed me right out of the room. He said it made me look like a mermaid. I knew what he meant and returned it the next day."

Abby, a mother of two sons, told me that for one son's wedding, she was so exhausted by the search for the right dress that her sister stepped in and bought her a chiffon horror, a dress she never wore again. But for the other son's wedding, she bought a purple suit that "she wore to death."

Maybe for Someone Else, But Not for You
"It's not what you wear; it's who you are."—Michele Slung

Karen liked the gray linen dress she had worn to her first son's wedding so much that she wanted to wear it again when her second son was getting married. "No, Mom," he said, and Karen understood. It was important to him that his mother find that special dress for his wedding, just as she had done for his brother's. Whenever possible, it is nice for you to show your son the dress. Yes, you are asking for his approval. But then again, it is his wedding. Wouldn't it be wonderful if on that wedding day, he could look at you and say, "Mother, you look beautiful."

Be careful when you tell salespeople that you are the mother of the groom. They may lead you to dresses that are decked out in feathers or aglow with sequins. If you buy a dress that you like for the occasion but you know you are unlikely to wear it ever again, you can donate it to Goodwill or to your local high school drama department. They are always looking for costumes.

From Image to Reality

As you try on one dress after another, you become acutely aware of your hips, your bust, your neck, your arms, your age, your courage—and your budget. You soon discover that finding the best dress is discovering who you are. As Laura says, "I went from an image of myself as a serene beauty through the images of myself as a woman of wealth and property that the stores and boutiques offered me. Finding the best dress for me was learning how to say 'No.' No beige, no long jacket, no padded shoulders, no sleeveless, no Peter Pan collar, no beads. Maybe for someone else, but not for me."

Accessory Time

Jewelry, shoes, handbag. You've bought the dress, but that's only the beginning. You might want to discuss your accessories with the bride.

For jewelry, pearls usually work. They are simple, beautiful, elegant, and will go with every outfit. But Jean didn't want to wear pearls at her son's wedding. She wanted to wear an antique necklace that had been in her family for years. The bride's mother, however, insisted that she wear pearls for the look of the procession and for the formal pictures. "All the women in the wedding procession will wear pearls," she said. And Jean wore pearls.

In an event that should speak to sharing and union, the bride's mother was still controlling the wedding. The story ended happily, however, with Jean ultimately having her moment. At the reception, she took off her pearls and put on her necklace of choice. Again, as in many situations that will arise, sometimes you have to say yes to something you don't really want. Sometimes you can negotiate differences, and sometimes at just the right moment your turn will come.

As far as handbags go, you don't need one. You will want your hands to be free, maybe just to carry a handkerchief, which you will surely need at some point. Shoes should be comfortable but usually aren't. Make sure you have the right size and consider comfort over style. Remember you will be walking down the aisle slowly and gracefully; you don't want to wobble on heels that are too high. You may also be standing during the ceremony. If there is a reception line, you will surely be standing in it. It's the standing that really tests the comfort of your shoes. And, after all that standing, you want to be able to dance at the reception.

And the Men

Most of the attention goes to the women in the party. But if you're married, your husband needs equal time to talk about his outfit. He has probably listened to you and evaluated your choices endlessly. Now it's his turn. He is also eager to look his best, and he needs your help and your time to get him there.

Men have many more choices today than they used to have. Depending upon the time of day in which the ceremony takes place, the limits of black and white have stretched. Shirts can be blue or lavender, with ruffles, spread collars, wing tips, or no collars at all. Cummerbunds allow for more colors, even for plaids. Ties? Well, it all depends on the shirt.

Meredith's son, the groom, chose a double-breasted tuxedo jacket, white shirt with studs, black bow tie, and patent leather shoes for himself and for the men in his wedding party. But his father, Phil, was not pleased with the choice. He argued that a double-breasted jacket with a notched collar would make him look short. He didn't own a tuxedo, and he hated the thought of wearing a rented one. He pleaded for his beige suit. But this was an evening wedding, and the party would be dressed formally. No question, he had to wear a tuxedo.

"Even so," Meredith said, "Phil asked why he couldn't select a single-breasted jacket. It would look good on him and make him look taller. It seemed reasonable." He said, "If you can wear a dress of your choice and don't have to match the bride's mother, why can't I pick my own clothes?"

A single-breasted jacket with a shawl collar made all the difference for Phil. "Since the wedding was being held 250 miles away from here," Meredith said, "Phil also wanted his measurements to be taken at the store where the other men were getting their suits instead of having his measurements taken at our local tuxedo rental store and then sent on. That way he could be fitted properly and be able to talk to the man who was taking his measurements and making the alterations. He wouldn't have to worry about miscommunications. We didn't need to get there and find a jacket that was too big, a waist that was too tight, pants that ballooned in the seat." A very good idea.

Men also need to have the opportunity to look at themselves in the mirror and watch the transformation. It's not just a woman's thing. Men, too, enjoy the fun of trying on and picking the right costume, including the shirt, the studs, the shoes, and, of course, the black dress socks—which they probably forgot to bring, if, in fact, they ever owned any.

The Whole Is Greater Than the Sum of Its Parts

It's hard to minimize this particular shopping expedition. You will be on view. You want to shine but not outshine the bride. You want everyone to compliment you on your good taste and good looks. You want your son to be proud of you. Here are the basics:

- First, talk to the bride and her family about colors.
- If you're lucky, you will recognize the right dress soon and buy it. If not, relax with the journey.
- Take along a friend, and don't let salespeople intimidate you.

- Buy a dress that will make it possible for you to walk, sit, stand, and move with ease and grace. Buy a dress that you can dance in, a dress that will allow you to hug and kiss people.
- Make sure you have chosen comfortable shoes.
- Always keep in mind that you are wearing the dress; the dress is not wearing you. The dress isn't walking down the aisle. You are.

Keep these tips in mind, and you'll look and feel beautiful on your son's—and your—special day.

II.

Down to the Wire

Way, way back in time, when your son first told you he was getting married, the wedding date seemed like a tiny speck on the horizon, an astronomical date for the next eclipse. But suddenly, it's unimaginably upon you, along with the rush of things that still need to be done, settled, arranged so that you can move easily on that Great Day and look beautiful.

Make a List

There are just enough lax days here to make you worry about everything. Did you forget to do something? Are you supposed to do something? What can you do to calm down? Making a checklist will alleviate nine out of ten of your anxieties. Talk to your son, your future daughter-in-law, and her mother. Together, all of you can draw up a checklist of everyone who has to be called, everything that has to be reviewed—flowers, limos, food, tuxedo rentals, and so on.

Never assume anything.

Do the men know when they can pick up their tuxedos? Louise's brother, who was driving in from Vermont, assumed that one of the groomsmen would pick up his tuxedo when they picked up theirs. But he hadn't asked anybody to do so. No one did. When he arrived on Sunday morning, the store was closed. No tuxedo for him. His mother finally located a neighbor, someone tall and big enough from whom he could borrow a navy blue suit.

Include your car in that checklist. Make sure that it's working well. One father I know was about to pick up his tux when his car wouldn't start. He had to use his wife's, which then forced her to scour the neighborhood to borrow someone else's car so that she could pick up her aunt at the hairdresser's, meet a cousin who was arriving at the airport in an hour, and tend to everybody's last-minute needs on the morning of the wedding.

Once you have drawn up a master checklist with the family, have the list divided so that everyone end up with an assignment. Then ask one person (possibly you) to be in charge of checking the lists—to see that everyone has touched base with everything. Just making such a list will relieve the tension in the air. It will give everybody something to do and use up all that restless energy. Most important, every task will get attended to.

Brunch?

How can you manage to be a gracious hostess to all the people who are coming to your son's wedding and still find time to spend with special friends who may be traveling great distances to be with you? Should you make a breakfast for just your friends and relatives the morning after the wedding? Is that expected? Or is that redundant, after the rehearsal dinner and the reception?

The rehearsal dinner will bring everyone together. So will the wedding reception. But those occasions are with all those other people, not with your special friends and family.

It is not necessary to make a brunch, and no one will think less of you if you don't. But if it's practical, casual, and doesn't involve you in too much planning and more tension, this meal can provide at least some of the time you're looking for—a time not squeezed in between other events. Besides, it's a nice "coming down" time for your guests, many of whom may not be quite ready to take off and may want some informal time to shmooze with you. Be sure to invite people ahead of time so they can make their travel arrangements accordingly and you can know how many will be able to stay.

Things Over Which You Have No Control

About two weeks before the wedding, you will find yourself listening avidly to weather reports. The weather is one more thing to worry about. Everybody wants the sun to shine, to be able to say, "What a lovely day for a wedding." On the other hand, you need to cover all bases. Isn't it common knowledge that "the sun never shines on a happy bride?" What are you going to do? Pray for rain? Not if you're having an outdoor reception. During those few days, you will develop a keen sense of the daily cloud formations as they move across Canada. You will study the weather channel, steel yourself for rain, and pray for sun.

Making Sure That Everyone Is Happy

Although you're happy that many of your friends and neighbors are coming to the wedding, there's another side of friendship that can be especially demanding at this time. Try to be patient with your friends. People will call you for directions even though they were enclosed with the invitation. Someone will ask you to arrange a ride for her even though she knows who's coming and is perfectly capable of making her own calls. Someone else wants to know where to rent a car. Of course he could look it up in the telephone book. Don't be surprised or impatient to find yourself in charge of solving other people's problems.

Another matter will insinuate itself. Almost always at a wedding, there will be a guest who requires special handling: a physical, emotional, or dietary problem—someone who needs attention or extra care.

For me, it was my husband Arnold's eighty-six-year-old Aunt Harriet, who called a week before the wedding to say she couldn't come. She had never been an easy person for us to deal with, but now in her old age, she had become increasingly demanding and arbitrary. She said she had no clothes to wear, that it was painful for her to walk because she had fallen last December, that it was just too hard for her to come. But Aunt Harriet was the matriarch of the family. She had outlived Arnold's parents and mine, and we both felt the wedding would not have been complete without her. She had to be there, in some way to stand for all of them.

We made a special trip to see her and to make it virtually impossible for her to refuse us. It was hard work, but we went through her closet with her, found the right dress and shoes to match. She wore only heavy rubber-soled sneakers. "I have to have rubber soles. I don't want to have another fall." But on a back shelf in her closet, I discovered a perfectly fine pair of beige shoes with rubber soles. And an identical pair of black ones. She hadn't worn them in years, but all they needed was polishing. The physical problem of getting her to the wedding was solved; my husband's cousins would drive her.

Aunt Harriet was my problem. You will probably have your own variation of Aunt Harriet, someone who can't move around easily or who has other restrictions. Make sure the hotel, church, or catering hall has an elevator or ramps. Be aware of any of your guests' special needs and how best to accommodate them.

Yes, it is your son's wedding. You want to be filled with only the joy of the occasion and to have a wonderful time, but you don't always know what's going to make you happy until you are actually there in the moment and experiencing the day. In the process of solving problems, like the one of bringing Aunt Harriet to the wedding, you gradually feel better and better. After all, isn't this what Zen is all about?

Resolving Problems Brings Out the Best in You

Just when the little problems seem to be solving themselves, and you feel that everything is going well, something always happens to humble you. It's a reminder that in this world of hurricanes and snowstorms, of people and personalities, there are always some new lessons in dealing with the unexpected. You will emerge, as a result, shining and resilient and more confident of yourself than ever before.

Take Jennifer, whose son disappeared the night before his wedding. He hadn't left his family or his future bride any note explaining where he was going. But when he showed up at four in the morning on his parents' doorstep explaining that he'd been just driving around and thinking, Jennifer did not reprimand or scold him. She simply comforted him by telling him that everyone has doubts, even the bride, but that it would all work out. Then he came in, and they were both able to get some rest.

A Quiet Time with Your Son

Find a time to be with your son before he becomes the groom. He may need you. Maybe you can have lunch or breakfast—a private time for the two of you. Of course you will talk about the wedding, but you may also be giving him an opportunity to talk to you, to ease his stress and calm his nerves. He has had his share of bachelor parties, of talk and back-slapping from all sides. He knows that this is probably the most important step he will ever take in his life. In between the laughter and the good wishes, he also needs a quiet moment to reflect on what's happening to him. He needs to talk to someone who has always been his best listener—his mother.

Addressing Arguments

For Jessica, the unexpected happened when she invited her son Alec and future daughter-in-law, Corinne, to have dinner with her brother, his wife, and a few close friends from out of town. They had never met Corinne, and Jessica wanted them all to meet each other informally before the wedding. Alec showed up but without Corinne. "Corinne will be a little late. We had a slight misunderstanding," he said, "but she'll be here soon."

Jessica wondered if they had had an argument. What kind of a misunderstanding would prevent her future daughter-in-law from coming to dinner, especially when she knew that Jessica's close family and friends would be there? After several minutes,

Alec excused himself to check on Corinne. Jessica described the painful waiting as everyone continued talking, trying hard to be casual as if there was nothing out of the ordinary happening.

"Alec came back," she said, "and tried to smooth things over. He stammered his way through the explanation that he thought it was still possible that Corinne might be able to join us. But we should go ahead and have dinner. He smiled and had another beer.

"I was mortified, deeply embarrassed—for my son, for myself, and for everyone in the room. Everyone wanted to know why Corinne wasn't there, but they were all too polite to ask. After dinner, the party broke up, and then I did something I had never done before." Jessica said. "I asked no questions. I just said, 'Good night,' and hugged Alec."

Everybody's tension level rises on the days just before the wedding—that includes the bride, the groom, the families involved, and you, too. Recognize your tension, and respect its presence. That may very well keep you from overreacting.

Of course, you have also been scanning the relationship between your son and his chosen bride ever since the two of them decided to get married. Maybe you heard a word here and there or a story of something that she said or did. You've wondered if her temperament and personality and his likes and her dislikes would really work together. But the feeling passed when you watched them holding hands and had a good sense of them as a couple.

If they were just like each other, "two peas in a pod," that would make you feel comfortable. But you could also accept the idea that they might be different from each other. Differences can complement each other and enrich both parties. Isn't that how people grow? In Hebrew, the word used when a man chooses a wife is that he finds the "other," someone different from himself, almost implying an adversary.

But how should you react if you overhear an argument or witness a nasty scene between your son and his future wife? How do you control your instinct to protect your child? Your response will help to shape your relationship with your future daughter-in-law and your son for years to come.

The first reality check is to look at the situation from another perspective. In Jessica's case, that meant considering not what Corinne had done but, perhaps, what *Alec* might have done. As a mother, you only know your son in his relationship to you as a son. You have very little information about what he is like with other women and how he behaves with them.

The other new reality that you must accept is the fact that the problem is his to solve, not yours. You can no longer protect him from hurt and all bad things. He is not your little boy any more, and you are not his confidante. Yes, he still loves you, but he is in another place now. Whatever problems he has with the woman he has chosen to marry, they are his problems to solve by himself or with her. He and she are another synergism. And you are not part of that energy. That relationship has rules of its own, has its own history, its own dynamics, and has worked out its own method for solving problems.

The sequel to Jessica's story proves my point. The next morning, her son called from Corinne's house and said that Corinne would like to talk to her. "She apologized for not having been with us last night. There was a squabble between them. Some kind of a story she told me that I couldn't even keep track of. I was just so happy that she called I didn't ask her any questions."

There are two important lessons to be learned from this story. One is that the future husband and wife have to find their way to get over the bumps together. The fact that Alec and Corinne had stood side by side to make the call together demonstrated that they had managed to find their way. The second lesson is for the mother of the groom to say very little, not to take sides and not to ask too many questions. It isn't necessary for you to know the whole story of the argument or to tell your future daughter-in-law about all your hurt feelings or even to imply that it was no big deal. Sometimes it may be good for you just to be a sounding board between them, hearing each side but not taking either one.

This is a defining moment in your son's life as you allow him and his future wife to work out their own problems. It's also a defining moment for you as you practice separating yourself from your son's problems and begin a lifelong balancing act between being concerned and being involved. This is your first lesson in mother-in-law-hood.

What to Do in the Days Before the Wedding?

You've gone over your major checklist about all the important wedding things. Now you can make up your own personal list, making sure you have done everything you had to do and have everything you need to have. The more things you can check out, the less tension you will feel.

Have you bought the stockings to match your shoes or your dress? Are the earrings too much for the dress? You know the perfume you're going to wear, the lipstick and the nail polish. Do you really want a makeover at Bloomingdale's? Set your appointments for hair, nails, and makeup well in advance of the date so that you get the people you want to make you look the way you want. In many situations, you can arrange to have someone come to you the day of the wedding to do your hair and makeup. This might be a close friend who knows how to do these things. Aim to look like you—only a little better. Don't experiment with a new hairstyle or color.

Touch base with others. Take some time to call your future daughter-in-law and her mother. This is a good time just to say "How's everything going?" or "Anything I can do?" It's a very simple and tension relieving thing to do. It keeps people connected, and it gives everybody a chance to sigh.

Managing the Hours Before the Festivities

The time-management problem begins when you realize that you have nothing to do until the rehearsal and the rehearsal dinner. After all the built-up excitement, tension, and activity of the past few weeks and days, a sudden stop will feel strange, even disquieting. Bring along a good book, some knitting, or some crossword puzzles. Go to the gym and release all that adrenalin. Get a massage. Don't do what Emily did.

The following story has a moral to it.

Emily is a very well organized woman. She runs a small business and knows how to manage time. On the morning of the wedding rehearsal and the rehearsal dinner, she found herself with five or six hours and no obligation to do anything—but with an unbounded energy to keep moving, going, doing, fixing . . . something.

"So I decided to take a tour of center city Philadelphia, the Independence Hall area. It was not far from where the wedding was, and it was a place I was interested in seeing...someday. My mistake was in thinking that this would be a good day to go, that it would take my mind off everything, that it would relax me. Big mistake."

Emily had forgotten that it was also a holiday weekend, and she got caught in the middle of a huge traffic jam. "Although the concierge at the hotel had said it was just thirty minutes away, it took us an hour and a half to get to center city Philadelphia.

Once there, we found lines for the tour almost a city block long. I began to be nervous about time. I lost interest in the tour and wanted only to get back to the hotel. We were unfamiliar with the highways, so my husband, who was driving, kept losing his way. It was a nightmare. We drove up and down ramps, pulled into gas stations for directions, looped around again past the same signs, not knowing east from west, north from south.

Hot, exasperated, and angry with each other, we rushed to get dressed for the rehearsal and blamed each other for getting into the mess."

On this important weekend, you don't want to break out into a sweat. There will be enough unforeseen circumstances to deal with; you don't have to create them. You don't want to have a fight with your husband. You need him as your best friend. You don't want to squander your emotional capital. You will need to draw on it for the rehearsal and the rehearsal dinner. You can't relax by crowding your schedule to fill nervous spaces.

The Rehearsal Dinner and You

Wedding rehearsals never begin on time, and they always take longer than you think. Schedule the rehearsal dinner long enough after the rehearsal that you can participate in the rehearsal and still get to the restaurant early enough to make sure everything is just the way you want it to be. Have the flowers been arranged on the tables the way you want them? Are there enough chairs? Have there been any menu changes? And then there are always the guests who arrive early. Remember also that it has been three or four hours since you last checked your makeup and combed your hair. You need time to refresh and collect yourself.

The party begins before you're quite ready for it. From the time the first guest arrives, things move with incredible speed.

People come in. They kiss you; they kiss each other. Or they shake hands and introduce themselves to you and then kiss you. They see their long-lost friends and relatives and greet them with joy and much hugging and kissing.

You will probably never really know how good the food is at your rehearsal dinner because as the mother of the groom, the hostess of the party, you will be moving from table to table checking to see that people have enough to eat. Is anyone drinking too much wine? I remember one rehearsal dinner in which the father of the groom celebrated beyond reason and paid for it the next morning, looking pale and holding on to his wife's arm for dear life as he walked down the aisle beside her.

Be sure that someone brings a camera to the dinner. You will want lots of pictures of the bride and groom, of the bride's mother sitting next to your brother, of everybody waving or smiling up at you. Whenever you remember that rehearsal dinner, those pictures will come to mind, and you will once again hear the sounds of people laughing and talking or calling across the tables to each other. There is a level of sound to a successful party that tells you people are having a good time. You know it when you hear it. For an incredible few hours, you will find that you have really lost sight of the bride and groom. Don't feel guilty. This is your party, and it's important that you enjoy yourself.

Soon enough, the time passes. The guests blow kisses and wave goodbye, and the waiter will present you with the bill. Check it. The tip for service has probably been added; if not, don't wince at 20 percent. For most of the women I spoke to, the rehearsal dinner was worth every bit of it.

After the dinner, you can almost relax—and you should! You helped wherever and whenever you could to make your son's wedding a happy and beautiful event. And the very special piece of it that was your sole responsibility went well. Now you can look forward to the wedding.

The Countdown

At this point in the planning, you are now well prepared for your son's wedding—emotionally, intellectually, and practically, for all these reasons:

- The rehearsal dinner has gone well, just as you planned it.
- You have made a checklist with your son, the bride, and her family to go over everything connected to the wedding. And everybody knows what to do.
- You have made sure that all your guests' special needs, dietary as well as physical, can be accommodated.
- You've taken some private time with your son to walk him through his feelings and concerns.
- You've also called the bride and her mother just to say hello, to find out how they're doing—really just to connect.
- You have everything you need from head to toe, from perfume to powder, to create the mother of the groom you want to be.

- You have a full tank of gas in the car, which is in good shape in case you're needed to run errands.
- Now all you have to do is listen to the last-minute weather report.

Can you trust the forecaster, who has just promised clearing in the afternoon with sunshine tomorrow? Did he also say, "Stiff winds?"

12.

The Wedding

WHEN YOU WAKE UP ON the morning of the wedding, the first thing you check is the weather. After that you go back to bed, replaying the events of the day and the night before—the rehearsal and the rehearsal dinner. Unlike what you might have expected, the morning of the wedding can almost seem serene. But once you're out of bed, the events of the day unfold. Things go slowly at first and then move into fast forward.

In the Morning, Take a Deep Breath

Last night's rehearsal dinner, where so many of the wedding guests joined in and for which you were responsible, came off brilliantly. You also vividly remember yesterday's wedding rehearsal, in which you walked down the aisle, heard the music, watched all the players, and practiced your part in the wedding. You have the strangest sense that the wedding has already happened. Today is almost after the fact.

But at some point in all of these preparations and celebrations, you will find yourself swept up in a tide of emotion. At that very special moment, the implications of the event really hit you once more. It might happen when your son first announces his engagement, on the morning of his wedding, or (most likely) during the wedding ceremony itself. When it happens, take a deep breath. Understand that in the course of such an important emotional event, you are bound to have moments like these. But also know that you will emerge from them with newer insights about yourself and your new relationship to your son.

The Kite As Metaphor

"With each twist of the ball of twine there is a sadness that goes with the joy, because the kite becomes more distant, and somehow you know it won't be long before that beautiful creature will snap the lifeline that bound you together and soar as it was meant to soar—free and alone."
—Erma Bombeck

For me, it happened during the rehearsal. Maybe it was the swelling of the music or the sunlight beaming through the chapel windows, but I felt my son's presence very close to me holding my hand tightly as we walked down the aisle together. When we got to the steps of the altar, he suddenly let go of my hand and stopped before the altar as the minister asked. And I continued to walk. Past him, up the few steps, and to the far right of the altar where I had been told to stand. For me, this was a metaphor. I didn't know what other moments the ceremony itself would offer me; I only knew that this separating of hands had been the moment of the wedding for me.

This visceral understanding will also happen to you as you realize that your son's wedding is not about his separation from you, but about your separation from him.

Getting Ready

There are even a few halcyon moments before the wedding. By this time, most of the serious problems have been solved, and neither rain nor snow will interfere with this wedding date. Last-minute emergencies will always pop up—a hole in the bride's veil, the best man's sprained ankle, the minister's delay in traffic. Take a deep breath again. Don't panic. Most of these events will be totally out of your control. But rest assured that everything will all work out because it must, and your wedding guests will never know there was a problem.

Depending on when the ceremony is scheduled, you may even have time for a simple breakfast with a friend. Don't overdo anything—not the food or the social conversation. A big breakfast, even lots of coffee, is dangerous; too much talk takes from your energy and is exhausting. The key word is *conservation.*

One of the best parts of the day is getting dressed. Give yourself plenty of time because it can be fun to savor the transformation. It's nice if you can include something personal, something mystical to your outfit. The bride wears something old, something new, something borrowed, and something blue, but you can also wear something that has special significance for you. It might be a bracelet or a pair of earrings. I wore the pearls my husband had given me as a gift for our wedding. Wearing them to my son's wedding gave me a sense of continuity and, also, a little bit of magic—as if they might bring my son good luck, too.

Leave enough time to put on makeup and do your hair. Don't rush the eye makeup, and don't apply too much. Be sure you use the waterproof kind. If your husband isn't there to give you an approving look, ask a friend to check you over to make sure no threads are hanging and the tag in the back of the blouse is tucked in. Someone else helping you to dress or just being there to relieve your tension will give you that added measure of security about how you look.

But before you leave for the limo, make sure you have a beautiful handkerchief somewhere—up your sleeve, in a pocket, in the purse you may be carrying, or in your hand.

Enjoy the Gathering Together

It's wise to arrive early at the chapel, about thirty minutes before the guests. You need to be alone in the place of the wedding for just enough time to hold the event in your hands before everybody rushes in and becomes a part of it. The chapel, the tall green plants and grasses, white astilbe and peonies, bouquets of flowers decorating the pews. The sun streaming in through the tall windows warming the altar and the room. You want a moment to absorb the scene before it rushes by. A montage of pictures will shortly be flashing up for you— suddenly now, then suddenly becoming memory. Of course you will have a photographer there, and many guests will be taking pictures, but you will also be storing up one image after another in rapid succession. Try to live in this moment. Don't think about the dinner last night or the reception coming up. Just try to live in what is actually happening to you now.

These will be the pictures in your memory with an emotional overlay that still shots can never capture. If it's a sunny day, the scene will look as if it has been lifted out of a picture book. In a formal wedding, the little flower girls will come running by in their long white dresses; the ring bearer, probably dressed like a medieval page, will be reaching toward his mommy for help. If the bride and groom agree, it's always nice to have children included in the wedding ceremony. Unreliable performers though they may be, they add a country charm to the scene and make you think you're in a French painting.

I heard a sermon once in which the minister said that we all live in three times: anticipating an event, experiencing the event, and remembering the event. "The trouble with most people is that they spend too much time anticipating and remembering instead of living in the event." Live this day. Live this event.

More cars keep coming, emptying out people who come across the lawn or up the path to the chapel. It's very much like a community coming together. You remember all those phone calls back in December and the details of February and March. The invitation. How would it look? What would it say? Who would come? Those once-unfamiliar names now have faces that you've come to recognize. And now they're all here, smiling, waving, saying a brief hello, and sweeping past you to get a front-row seat.

Bernice stepped out of the chapel to greet her friends and saw her son in his tuxedo walking up the steps to meet her. "He was so incredibly handsome. I couldn't help remembering this broad-shouldered, distinguished, confident young man in the Nehru jacket he wore when he was ten, and the tweed jacket I bought him for his first job interview. I suddenly felt like crying, but I wasn't sad. It was really a surge of joy. I just hugged him."

In such a juggernaut of emotion, you either have to burst out laughing or burst out crying.

Much too quickly, you hear the prelude music. You watch the ushers lead people to their seats. Then the bride arrives, and the ushers close the doors to the chapel so that the congregation won't see her before they're supposed to. At this moment, you probably don't see her as your future daughter-in-law. She is simply a beautiful woman. It's one thing to see bridal gowns on mannequins in Fifth Avenue shops. It's quite another to see this most spectacular of women's dresses on the woman herself. It's a fantasy-like moment, ultimately worth all the stress and money that went into it. But no matter what she wears, the great white dress, a simple beige suit, or jeans, it's really true that all brides are beautiful. The occasion is transformative.

The Bridal Procession

The traditional wedding ceremony has its history in the Middle Eastern bridal procession with a veiled bride, worn to protect her from evil spirits, and her handmaidens and flower girls and music, with the onlookers craning to see her, to "ooh" and "aah" at her beauty. Today's ceremonies are a blend of ancient and modern rituals responding to the wishes of many cultures and generations, rich with the symbols of many faiths.

While You Wait

While you wait silently for the ceremony to begin, you can distract yourself by observing the bridal party, which is probably separated from you and standing together in a corner of the anteroom. Who are these bridesmaids and groomsmen, these young men and women specially picked by the two young people who are about to marry each other? What is their unique relationship to the bride and groom? Are they supposed to protect them? Are they symbols of loyalty and trust standing by their closest friends in this holy hour? Are they the young stewards who are most qualified to usher one of their own from one time in life to another?

Who Walks in the Procession?

Everything that seemed so awkward at the rehearsal yesterday moves easily today. Yesterday, everyone was so casual, so friendly, so full of jokes and fun, trying on their new roles and stumbling through their lines. Yesterday, everyone was trying on the look of the wedding. Today, the look fits them perfectly. Waiting for their turn to go on, they now seem so assured, sophisticated, and confident of their movements.

And you? You know what to do. You practiced it yesterday. The minister assigned everyone the order of the procession. Mother and father of the groom go first. Often the groom enters with his parents. But he can also enter by himself. Then the mother of the bride comes in either, alone or accompanied by a son. Then the bridal procession itself: the flower girls sprinkling the way, the maid of honor, if one has been designated, the bridesmaids, the ring bearer, and ultimately, the bride brought in by her father, by a brother if her father isn't there, or by some other stalwart member of the family—usually male.

The people who will be part of the procession, as well as the order of the procession, is often negotiable, except, of course, for the ending with the bridesmaids and the bride. Different people make different decisions about whom they want to include in the procession. You can talk about this with the minister. Donna wanted her sister and her brother-in-law to be included in the procession, to be honored in some special way because they had supported her and her children after her divorce and during a difficult time in her life. The minister and

Donna agreed, along with Donna's son and future daughter-in-law, to have them enter during the prelude music when the congregation was seated.

In another wedding, the bride was not brought in by her father, who was divorced from her mother, but by her mother's partner who had helped to nurture her during her growing-up years.

Now It's Your Turn

While you are waiting for the ceremony to begin and probably absorbed in your own thoughts, you suddenly discover that someone has silently and magically opened the doors. You see the congregation waiting for you. The best man has unfurled the white carpet, just the way he was told to do yesterday at the rehearsal, and now you know that you are on. Everyone is standing and looking in your direction. Try as you might, it is a tense moment. You have been waiting in the wings, and, like all performers, you have been terrified of making a mistake and looking like a fool—tripping on your dress, not walking in time to the music, giggling with embarrassment, stumbling over your lines. It's called stage fright.

The music begins, and you are now part of the performance. As you step out onto the carpet, the fear and anxiety will melt away. Waiting is always full of tension. Action releases it. You know where to go and how to get there with grace and ease.

It is a short distance, but a long walk. Some people may favor a half-step, but that's just one more thing to remember, and it creates a more studied look. You don't want to take short steps or long strides. You just want to take it slowly, careful not to rush ahead of the music.

Push your shoulders back and hold your stomach in. Yes, you can smile at people but resist the temptation to wave. You don't have to stare beatifically into space. Make it a quiet smile, not quite as broad as the one you wear when someone is taking your picture. You know it's a little put on. You want to remind everyone that this person walking down the aisle is really you, and, despite the enigmatic look on your face, you are really happy. At the same time, you don't want to be distracted by the smiling faces of friends and lose the beat.

You know your assigned place, and you take it. Maybe the usher leads you to your seat in the first pew, or you may walk with your son up the steps to your designated place on the altar.

Time to Relax and Enjoy the Wedding

It's good to be the mother of the groom because you usually get to go first. Then you can feel relieved that you have successfully navigated the long aisle and enjoy watching the rest of the procession.

Even though you have been to many weddings, and you have seen plenty of flower girls and ring bearers, these children coming down the aisle in front of you will most likely be one of the most precious sights you have ever seen. The little girls clinging to each other, carrying baskets but barely bold enough to scatter the petals. The ring bearer walking bravely alone.

All those decisions, made here and there over weeks and months from kitchen phones and around dining room tables.

The flowers, the bridesmaids, the dresses they would wear, the music, the little children, the bride. The whole is much greater than the sum of its parts. You find yourself watching not just a procession but a pageant filled with colors and sounds that fairly lift you off the ground. You can afford to smile now. Nothing could stop you as you watch the bride come down the aisle.

She is both truth and mystery. Yes, you know some of her likes and dislikes. You also know a little bit about her personality. You cannot help feeling proud of your son's choice. But, unless she is someone who has grown up with your son and whom you have known for a long time, you are still learning about her. All those old questions are wrapped in a white veil. You have been on an emotional roller coaster for months leading to this unique space and time, when all the tensions seem to have resolved themselves into one perfect and whole moment.

And then your son steps forward to claim his bride and to bring her up the steps to stand with him. It is indeed, as the minister said at the rehearsal, "the triumph of the obvious." In earlier times, the act of the groom taking the bride's hand signified the marriage. It is a physical statement. You watch your son with a new respect as he smiles and assumes the mystery of his future.

The Ceremony

If your son and his fiancée asked you to do a reading at their wedding, now is your moment. Remember there are no set rules to the kinds of selections you may choose as your reading.

Readings can be personal testimonies to the bride and groom or inspirational pieces. You don't have to memorize what you want to say. Whatever you choose to read, have it typed or printed on an easily read sheet of paper. You don't want to lose it, forget it, or have it all crumpled up so that you can't read it. Leave that piece of paper in the safe hands of the minister, who will be sure to bring it with him to the wedding.

We had three different readings in our son's wedding service. The bride's aunt read a poem her husband had written, an epithalamium, which spoke of the vision of happiness and love and hope that the sight of the wedding couple evokes in all our hearts. We rejoice anew, and our belief in love returns.

I was next. I chose a passage from Anne Morrow Lindbergh's book, *Gift from the Sea*. She explains why the purity of feeling that marks the beginning of love doesn't remain like that always. Life complicates love, she says. Children complicate love, careers complicate love, daily living together changes love. But she warns us not to be afraid of that change. Relationships must change; that's part of living and growing. When you love someone, you must know that you don't always love them in the same way and that there is nothing wrong with the ebb and flow of feelings. Lindbergh writes about the web of loyalties and interdependencies and shared experiences that make up marriage. And then she returns to the importance of that original pure feeling, the romantic love that first brings people together, the wellspring of the relationship, the feeling they must return to from time to time, the "rainbow" that leaps across all the other bonds uniting people in marriage.

Then my husband spoke. He had written a special piece that he called "The Courage to Love." Addressing his remarks directly to the bride and groom, instead of to the audience, he told them that love was not a tranquil pond with lilies floating on it. Instead, happiness was dynamic and full of controversy, conflict, and brushfires. So, to love someone means to be willing to resolve conflicts, put out brushfires, and, by doing so, deepen the commitment to each other. The courage to love, he said, means not only to share the most intimate aspects of your life and vulnerability but also to be able to hold back rash words, angers, and solemn confessions that relieve you more than they help your partner.

The readings we chose were not only relevant to the couple about to be married; we believed they mattered to our congregation of friends and relatives—single, married, divorced, and widowed.

The Vows Make It Real

"To have and to hold from this day forward, for better for worse, for richer for poorer, in sickness and in health, to love and to cherish, till death us do part."—Book of Common Prayer

With This Ring I Thee Wed

"With this ring . . ." Your son takes the ring and slips it on the bride's finger. You may find yourself a little breathless at that moment. Up till now, you have had a sense of unreality, of being part of a play—with actors, costumes, and scenery. But the ring makes it real. Hearing your son take his vow, and seeing your son with the ring of marriage on his finger, brings everything into focus. He is married. The mundane language that follows, proclaiming that the laws of the state declare this marriage to be legal sounds anti-climactic, certainly after the fact.

The kiss, the blessing, the trumpets, and the organ. The recessional music. The end.

Rewind

It's all over, and you want to go back and do it again. This time, you want to really see and hear everything that happened. Of course, your mind knows what has happened, but the rest of you has not yet had time to catch up.

When you hear the chimes ring out in the bell tower, however, you will recognize the moment you have been waiting for. This is the moment when all the separate pieces come together, and, from deep inside you, the feelings resonate. This is it, the moment when you will reach for your handkerchief. In the words of an old Hebrew adage, "When the heart is full, the eyes overflow."

13.

The Reception

YOU NEED AN INTERIM TIME to quiet down, to shake everyone's hands, to acknowledge how beautiful everything was, and to get ready for the reception, which is coming up and in which you still have an important role to play. A receiving line is another one of those good old customs. It's hard to go from the emotion of the wedding ceremony to the burst of talk and energy of the reception. If the bride and groom choose to have a receiving line, it is a good way to make the emotional transition and to allow people to greet them personally and tell them how wonderful it all was. It is also a good time for you to introduce yourself to members of the bride's family and friends whom you have not yet met, a relatively quiet time before the rush of the reception sweeps everybody up and it becomes difficult for you to meet new people.

Between the Ceremony and the Reception

With or without a formal receiving line, the time immediately after the ceremony is the perfect space for collecting yourself and shifting your focus from all those serious reflections to hugs and kisses and demonstrations of public affection. It's like the exhale after a deep sigh. You greet your friends, relatives, and all those people whose names you don't remember but who have come to the wedding and who have shared the occasion with you. It's also the perfect time for picture taking. The photographer will certainly be there and so will all those friends with their digital cameras.

If you are in a receiving line, remember to wear comfortable shoes. Alma told me how she suffered. "I was wearing elegant gray pumps with a high thin heel. I stood there smiling and greeting everyone while the lower part of my body, from the waist down, slowly turned numb. First I shifted from one leg to the other, and then the pain started shooting up my leg into my back. I could not have moved into the rest of the day if my husband hadn't thought ahead and urged me to bring along another pair of gray shoes. He thought I would need them for walking on the grass at the reception. I needed them to survive."

Your Role at the Reception

There are three parts to this big day: getting ready for the wedding, participating in the wedding service, and cohosting the reception after the wedding. So far, you have run the emotional gamut this day, and you've only gone two-thirds of the way. From early morning tension, to the powerful realization of a big change in your life, you have an overwhelming sense of pride and joy as you join your son in this ceremony of change.

You're ready to enjoy the third part of the day—the reception. The wedding reception is a unique party for the mother of the groom. It's your party, and it's not your party. You are both guest and host.

As a Guest

As a guest, you can enjoy the setting, the music, and someone else serving you the hors d'oeuvres. After the intensity of the wedding, the reception provides essential nourishment for body, mind, and spirit. You need food to replace your exhausted energy—like after a fever. Yes, talk to your friends, but be sure you eat along with them as the servers wind in and out of the guests. Otherwise, you will be hungry at the end of the night— and, worst of all, you will never know how delicious that twist of shrimp was that everybody was reaching for.

Enjoy being a guest at your own party. Receptions are usually held at the home of the bride's parents, in a restaurant, a catering hall, a hotel ballroom, or a country club. In most cases, the reception is not held in the home of the mother of the groom. Therefore, you don't have to worry about cleaning the house, repairing the fence, or providing for parking. A relief!

As a Host

But as the host, you share some of the responsibility for making sure that everyone is having a good time, taking care of your guests, introducing people to each other, and seeing that everyone is comfortable and has something to eat.

You probably didn't have to do any of the cooking. But you probably shared the expense and have been part of the planning for this event, so you have more than a guest's interest in seeing that this is a good party. Unlike the other guests at the reception, you're also a hostess, and you will find yourself quickly assuming that role. The following tips describe how to do it right:

- Walk among the guests making sure they are eating well and that their glasses are filled. Also be sure there are beverages for people who don't drink alcohol.

- You have a role to play in the success of this party. Leave your circle of warm friends and introduce yourself to some of your son's and now your daughter-in-law's friends. Not only will they be pleased to meet you, ("Oh, you're Jeffrey's mother! How nice to meet you."), but you will also get a new and fresh look into your son's and daughter-in-law's lives when you meet their friends.

- And then there's the bride's family, her mother's friends and neighbors, who were not invited to the rehearsal dinner and many of whom you've never met. So far, they've just been names that you've heard mentioned. Extend yourself to them and thank them as they congratulate you. Talk to them so that they become more than a name to you and so that you become a person they recognize.

- Assist guests who need your help, maybe members of the bride's family whom you have just met.
- Introduce members of the bride's family to members of your family, and stay with them for a while to see that the families are comfortably chatting with each other. Your role is to help make that happen.
- Make sure that your unattached friends are not standing alone.

While you are doing all of these things, you should also take some time to enjoy the panorama. There are lovely, relaxing moments as you watch the guests arrange and rearrange themselves in bright spots of color, the little children chasing after each other, your son in his tuxedo, and the bride floating around in a white bubble.

Feelings Are Complicated

You are "mother," which you understand, but you are also newly minted "mother-in-law," which you have yet to grasp. It's easy for you to hug your son in passing, but if you feel a trifle self-conscious doing the same thing in the same way with the same feeling to this young woman who is suddenly your daughter-in-law, don't worry about it. The relationship has only been made in a ceremony; it has yet to be made in time.

Dance at Your Son's Wedding

Music is the universal solvent. It helps to ease all the opposing elements into a sustainable mix. Music is the atmosphere that helps everyone breathe. It was a very thoughtful courtesy of one groom to ask several people the day before the wedding what music they would like played at the reception. An old uncle of the bride requested, "Don't Sit Under the Apple Tree with Anyone Else But Me," while the mother of the groom asked for "Love Me Tender."

Dance at your son's wedding. If you don't have a partner, find one. Dancing at weddings helps people loosen up, get exhausted and exhilarated. Husbands and wives finally have a chance to dance with each other again—whether the band plays rock and roll, Glenn Miller, the *hora*—or "The Pennsylvania Polka," as they did at a wedding I attended, where the groom's family was Polish. Then again, it might be Strauss waltzes, as at another wedding where the bride was a musician and all her friends from Julliard provided the music and everyone waltzed. Dancing lets you step into the rhythm of the party.

Dinner Is Served

Dinner is signaled when the music stops. Sometimes there are servers, sometimes a buffet, and sometimes tables are numbered and called in turn for people either to be served or to serve themselves. If the last option is your situation, let me give you a food advisory. When your table is called, stop talking to your friends and get in line or someone else will get in line twice, and you'll discover that there are no lamb chops left for the mother of the groom.

A Toast to the Bride and Groom
"May you live as long as you want and want for
nothing as long as you live."—Traditional

Happy Words for You to Say

Once the room is filled and people are seated, the joy of the occasion burbles over into toasts and blessings. There are traditional blessings over the bread usually said by a minister or an honored member of the family. Then the best man, usually, as toastmaster, salutes the couple with either a humorous or a serious toast. This time also offers a special opportunity for friends and relatives to stand up with a glass of whatever they choose to drink and honor the newlyweds with a toast to their health and future happiness.

You can fit into this space with ease. This is not a gender issue, not just a male moment. You can also raise a glass and give a toast. You can quote from a poem or tell a story that reveals something wonderful about your daughter-in-law, your son, or both—providing it's not so personal a story as to embarrass them and that it's general enough for all the other people in the room to understand and appreciate. You can simply wish the couple good fortune in your own words and in your own way.

Whatever you choose to say, be sure you have it written down and in front of you; standing up and speaking into a microphone can be unnerving. Just remember to make it short, relevant to the occasion, and something that everyone can enjoy listening to. Probably others will be next in line to toast, and although everyone in the room is happy for the bride and groom, they are also hungry.

What to Do When the Unexpected Happens

Everything can be going according to plan—a perfect meal, the best wines, continuous music. But human effort and will cannot control everything. The unexpected often happens. It's how you deal with it that matters.

It may rain, possibly a sudden downpour forcing everyone to cover up their wedding finery with raincoats and carry umbrellas as they leave the church for the reception. Have emergency rain gear in the car.

In one wedding, the groom's mother watched graciously as the bride's mother startled the guests by suddenly breaking into a belly dance. This was not an ethnic statement; she was not Egyptian or Tunisian. She was simply having a good time, and she knew how to belly dance. The mother of the groom knew the woman well, knew that she was an exotic person, and almost anticipated the moment. Although she found the dancing embarrassing, no one would ever have known it; she smiled benignly and applauded when the performance was over. Because she easily accepted the situation, she made it possible for her guests to accept and enjoy it and to applaud along with her.

At another wedding, the reception was being held outdoors. Eleanor expected mosquitoes and had prepared for them as best she could with mosquito repellent at every table. She even violated her environmental principles by having the grass sprayed. Huge citronella torches burned. If you live on the edge of the wetlands, and it is the end of May, the mosquitoes will come.

And like one of the ten plagues of Egypt, on cue, thousands of them descended at sunset. People swatted, flung their hands in all directions, and covered their heads with handkerchiefs. Some people laughed, others cried out, and everyone gasped when, as suddenly as they came, they left. The mosquitoes only stayed for about ten minutes, and they disappeared when the wind changed. Nobody was actually bitten. All that preparation must have helped. At least it discouraged the mosquitoes from hanging around.

Although you cannot prepare for every eventuality, you can think through logical scenarios that might occur. Keep in mind that "Life is what happens when you're making other plans."

The Cake-Cutting Ceremony

There is still one more ritual to go. When dinner is over, people will begin to drift. You want to remind them not to leave before the cake cutting, which will happen about an hour after the meal. This gives guests time to finish eating, maybe to dance a little more or visit people at other tables. You can help to gather people at the fringes for the cake cutting.

The great wedding cake—temples and towers and columns with silver bells and ribbons, it is a baker's imagination run wild. It might even be something that you or the bride and groom have made—a not impossible and very worthy undertaking. There are many recipes for this cake, which has a great deal of meaning to it. One recipe describes the alternating layers of white cake and fruitcake as symbols of virginity and fertility, sweetness and richness, light and dark—a promise of the future.

When the cake is finally finished, the result, iced and decorated with ribbons and flowers, makes a beautiful statement. It's a basic part of the celebration, white and ornate, dressed like the bride, very much a symbol of the wedding.

If the couple makes their own cake, you can give them, as a gift and your contribution to the cake, the essential figures of the bride and groom that go on top of the cake, the crowning achievement of the wedding fantasy.

The cutting of the cake is also a ceremonial act. Bride and groom cut the first few pieces together and then serve them to the guests. It's another way to share their joy and union. Usually, then, one of the servers appears to help cut the rest of the cake, to wrap the slices and serve them to the assembled guests. But you can also be there to pass around the plates and napkins.

Exit Husband and Wife

As the guests receive their slices of the cake, they also prepare to leave. For most people, it's the closing act of the play. But nobody leaves before the bride and groom. That's the real signal. Some time after the cake cutting, they disappear, only to return refreshed and looking bright and beautiful while all the rest of the party is gradually fading. Your son looks different to you now. He is no longer the groom; she is no longer the bride. They are husband and wife. You notice their wedding rings and how they hold hands. They look good together, as if they belonged that way. It is no longer "he" and "she"; it is "they" in your life—a new entity. They hug and kiss you and say goodbye and wave to everyone as they leave for their honeymoon. And, although you may feel a cool draft in a space where something else had once been, you can also anticipate that something equally wonderful will fill it.

The Party's Over, but Not for You

Try not to measure friendship by how late people are willing to stay. When it gets late, when it gets cold, when the food is gone, the party's over, and people need to get home. Be there for them when they leave and say, "Good night." As a gracious hostess, thank them once again for coming.

You may also be very tired, but something in you doesn't want the party to end. It all worked. The big things that had to go right did. You may think you are relaxing by now, but you are probably still wound up—the effects of the wine, the food, the dancing, and the echoes of all those different conversations.

Diana described that moment best as she looked out over the wedding scene. "Just a few couples were dancing or really just holding on to each other. The waiters were still serving. I felt like a character in a Fitzgerald novel. I knew this was the party of my lifetime. It made me wish I had had two or three more children."

Big weddings are an expense—of money, time, and energy. But they can be very gratifying experiences. Whether your wedding reception has been big or small, there will be rich memories to store up for future reflection and pleasure. Already you, too, are beginning to look at the wedding as part of the past.

You may stay for one last dance, one more cup of coffee, but try to leave before the musicians pack up. It's nice to keep the whole picture in your mind rather than to be left with the emptiness of the party's aftermath. You want to leave with the vividness of the evening in your body and soul. Before you leave the reception, however, be sure to make your goodbyes and thanks to the bride's parents and to any of her close relatives who are still there.

Afterthoughts

You will most likely be very tired and very awake when you return home or to your hotel room. The images of the wedding and the reception will be dancing in your head. Of course you'll see your son and his bride—two enchanting doll-like figures similar to those on top of the wedding cake. And you will also wonder what will happen to them as they step down from the top of the wedding cake—as they move from their wedding to their marriage.

Marriage. Such a complex relationship. You can't help thinking about marriage, and you fervently hope they will be able to manage the transition. How will your son move in easy tandem with the woman he has married? A whole set of questions suddenly takes on a new reality for you. If he wants to go here, and she doesn't, see this movie, eat eggplant, turn on the air conditioner? How to be alone? How to merge and yet be self? How will they react to the abrasions that close and daily contact inevitably bring? A disappointing response from him. A lack of response from her. An action that annoys, a reaction striking the flint that lights the fire. The things that no one can really tell them about before they're married, and even if someone tried, it wouldn't matter. They have to learn how to be married. It's the living of it that will teach them. It's the living of it that will make them grow and care and matter to each other. Or not.

And so here you are, way past midnight, thinking thoughts you would never have taken the time to think about. But your son was married today, and he gave you a special gift, a bonus. It's the gift of reflection—the time to think deeply and honestly about your own life, about marriage, your marriage, your decisions. "For better or for worse," you cannot help lying there in the dark or sitting in a chair or looking over your shoulder into a mirror examining, accepting—and coming to terms with the choices you have made. Your son's wedding is not only an extraordinary event in his life; it's an illuminating one in yours.

14.

You're a Mother-in-Law!

MORNING COMES WHETHER YOU'VE SLEPT or not, and you don't want to stay in bed too long. You're happy and tired, but you still feel as if there are a few more things for you to do. There may be guests who need you, travel arrangements to be made, bills to be paid. The big event has taken place. The wedding is fresh in your mind, and you are beginning to absorb it. But mostly what you have to do is pick up all the emotional pieces left over from yesterday and put them together into the new picture of yourself. Yes, you are still your son's mother, but you have a new relative—a daughter-in-law. And you are no longer the mother of the groom. You have become a mother-in-law.

Talking Helps You Process the Event

Almost all you want to do this morning is to listen to people tell you once again what a wonderful time they had, how beautiful the bride and groom looked, how great the food was, the music, the service, the reception. Everything. In order to really grasp what has happened, you feel as if you want to relive the entire wedding. And that's a good thing.

The second time around, you process it with help from your friends. The sounds of their voices telling you all the things you want to hear help you very gently to unwind. Talking has a sort of double-whammy effect. You experience not only your own sense of joy at reliving the day, but the other person's pleasure at telling you about it. This must be what is meant by that old saying, "A joy shared is doubled."

Depending on where the wedding took place, you might be on the telephone, exchanging responses with friends and relatives; in a hotel lobby, greeting people as they come out of the elevators; or, if you have planned a brunch, checking on the arrangements, anticipating with pleasure the time you will have with everyone you have invited.

Talking to Friends

One word of advice when you come up to your friends—don't begin by asking them if they had a good time. Let them respond first. If you meet them in the hotel lobby, and they seem preoccupied with making their own arrangements for going home or with other details of their lives and don't spontaneously jump into your joy, take a breath and give them time to come through. If you ask whether they had a good time, and they say how "nice" everything was, you will never believe them, and you will feel less than yourself for asking.

Be certain that at the right time they will soon tell you how wonderful it all was.

Regardless of whether you have prepared a brunch or not, it's important for you to be with other people. Have breakfast with a few close friends or relatives; set up an informal, cozy situation in which you can all talk about the wedding.

Trudy told me how relaxing it was, after all the hype and excitement of the wedding, simply to walk into the hotel dining room for breakfast and have coffee with friends. She said, "Some of my guests were sleeping late; others had already left. But the ones who were having breakfast enjoyed talking with me. Everyone was so casual. We really appreciated the opportunity just to be together for another hour."

Talking to the Bride's Family

One thing you want to be able to do this morning is to call the bride's family and see if you can connect with them today. Any reason for getting together will do. Be assured they want to talk about the wedding, reliving and remembering all the precious moments just as much as you do. Talking about the event will not only help to make it real for you, it will also, eventually, help you move on to the next step.

Dealing with Feeling

With breakfast over, guests will be hugging and kissing and leaving. After all the partying and post-partying, you may feel tired, but you are still on a high wire. You're slowing down, but you're not quite ready to stop. You have been perched in a high place, and it is quite impossible to come down from there the very next morning. You cannot just breathe normal air, pick up your daily schedule, and walk into Monday—unless, of course, you have to go to work. Too much energy and emotion has been let loose. You need to have at least another day between the wedding and the days thereafter. You almost have a physical need to keep moving, some activity to fill the vacuum. It would have been wise to plan a trip to Bermuda.

After our son Michael's wedding, my husband and I were restless and tired, but we thought we could use some of that leftover energy to do something on our way home. We really just needed a place to stop and some time to recoup.

We stopped at an inn and decided to take a nap. When we woke up at seven-thirty, we washed, got dressed, and came down for some comfort food—roast turkey, sweet potatoes, and cranberry sauce.

I watched a young couple at the next table trying to please as well as feed their little boy, who must have been no more than two years old. It was hard for them to keep him seated long enough to eat his dinner. Finally the young mother stopped trying to hold him in his chair and let him roam the dining room. He didn't bother anybody, and he was happy. A little unsteady on his feet, he walked around the tables and then into the hallway under the watchful eye of his mother, who saw him about to climb the stairs and ran after him. "Be careful, Michael," she said. "Be careful. Don't get hurt."

My hand reached up to my throat. I thought of my own son Michael and almost cried out.

Life Is a Metaphor of Change
"Life's picture is constantly undergoing change. The spirit beholds a new world every moment."—Rumi

Moving into the Future

Don't worry if you get teary. The confluence of all those emotions will come to a head at one point. For months you have experienced a range of emotions—happy, sad, nervous, excited.

This has been a big and an important time in your life—a time of significant change. Recognize it. And respect it. Your son has changed, and your relationship to him has changed. In a way your son is like that little boy I saw climbing up the steps, with a whole new world opening up in front of him. Your son is also learning how to take steps, how to move into his new role as husband and into his life as a married man. You are like that mother standing at the foot of the steps, always concerned about his safety but with hands off.

Daughter-in-Law and Mother-in-Law: A New Synergy

Just as your son has a new relationship in his life, with a woman who has now become his wife, you have a new relationship in your life, with that same woman who has now become your daughter-in-law. And you have a new title, a new identity to comprehend—you are a *mother-in-law.*

You don't just *become* a mother-in-law. You grow into it. Although the title has suddenly been conferred upon you, like any other significant change in your life, you have to live it to know it.

Celebrate your new status. Forget the jokes and stereotypes. A relationship is defined by who you are and what you want to have in a relationship. Know that what you want to have happen between you and your daughter-in-law involves you as much as it involves her. If you want your daughter-in-law to be a part of your life, you will have to make her a part of your life. Call her, include her in your plans, share your stories with her, and let her share her stories with you. This is how to create the bond you seek. Things don't just happen; you help them to happen. The wedding prepared you in many ways, including these:

- In this wedding, you helped to solve problems and create an event that would please everybody. You learned how to suggest, compromise, and accept decisions.
- You invited her family into your life.
- You helped to find common ground when there were differences of religion, culture, or race.
- You shared expenses whenever possible and practical and offered financial help when needed.
- You participated in the wedding ceremony.

- You assumed some of the practical responsibilities involved in the wedding preparations.
- You have been listening to your son and his wife and have learned about their plans, arguments, concerns, and wishes. You are now aware of a new dynamic in your life; it's *their* lives together that now interest you. You want to hear about *them*, and what *they* are doing.

You don't have to learn how to be a mother-in-law. All along the way, by your actions, your involvement, your interest, and your responses, you have become one. Congratulations!

The Daughter-in-Law As Gift

"And when we find ourselves in the place just right. It will be in the valley of love and delight."—"Simple Gifts," a Shaker hymn, author unknown

About the Author

Sydell Rabin is a freelance writer, a writing consultant, and president of her own company, The Writing Associates, Inc.

Formerly a department head of English, her articles have appeared in many educational journals as well as in commercial magazines. Scholastic, Inc., published her textbook on a technique for teaching students how to write better and how to approach state testing with confidence and skill. Several of her commentaries have aired on NPR's *Morning Edition*.

She has received two federal grants. One focused on the teaching of writing by training teachers, developing curriculum, and establishing a writing center. The second, in collaboration with New York University and distinguished American poets, dealt with the teaching of contemporary poetry.

She has been a guest speaker and presenter for a variety of national and regional educational associations and has served as an adjunct staff member at Kean University, Rutgers, and Montclair.

In her spare time, she organized a local nature conservancy dedicated to the restoration of an Olmsted urban park. She and her husband, writer Arnold Rabin, divide their time between Ipswich, Massachusetts, and Martha's Vineyard.